Anthropologies

sightline books

The Iowa Series in Literary Nonfiction

Patricia Hampl & Carl H. Klaus, series editors

Acknowledgments

I began writing this book when both my mother and my mother-in-law were failing. They were both wonderful storytellers and keepers of family histories and so I had been listening to these stories for years, never dreaming I would ever shape them into a book or even that they would become a well out of which I could draw other memories. Their stories are, of course, filtered through my own consciousness, and so others may remember differently; the book is also full of stories of other people, as each of our lives, I believe, is composed of a web of interrelationships. Gathering and distilling these memories was a pleasure, almost effortless at times; the difficulty came in arranging and shaping them into a larger narrative.

For their generosity as readers, and for support in sustaining the project, I owe special thanks to many good friends: to Barbara Cully, who has been a muse for this project from the beginning; to Laura Berry and Christiane Buuck, who encouraged early versions; to Karen Brennan and Polly Koch, who gave me brilliant suggestions right when I needed them; and to Susan Roberts and Aisha Sabatini Sloan, who acted as first responders and sustained my confidence in the writing. To Fernando, not only for being a constant reader and good storyteller, but also for allowing me to tell his stories as I saw them, and to Michael and Kathryn for allowing me to weave the stories of their lives into my own. To Kathryn, for her photographs.

I also owe thanks to Joseph Parsons and Carl H. Klaus at University of Iowa Press for seeing the promise in the manuscript and for their careful reading and thoughtful guidance. To Charlotte Wright, Emily Burker, Jenny Bennett, and all the others who transformed the manuscript into a book. And, finally, to *Third Coast* for publishing my essay

"Susan and the Zunis," and, in doing so, bringing my work to Joe's attention.

Parts of this manuscript have been previously published, although in altered form or in earlier versions, in the following journals and I would like to thank them. As "Excerpts from *Anthropologies*" in: *Cue: A Journal of Prose Poetry*, vol. 3.1 (Winter 2006); *Thin Air* (Fall 2008); *Seattle Review*, vol. 2.1 (January 2009); *Back Stage Live* website (Summer 2010). As passages in longer essays in: "Clarity," *Cimarron Review* (Winter 2009); "Days of the Dead" *Sonora Review* (Spring 2011); "Notes from Prague," *Nimrod* (Spring 2011); "Shelter," *North American Review* (Fall 2010).

Finally, I would like to thank the University of Arizona Provost's Author Support Fund for its support.

sightline books

The Iowa Series in Literary Nonfiction

Beth Alvarado
Anthropologies

A Family Memoir

University of Iowa Press   Iowa City

University of Iowa Press, Iowa City 52242
Copyright © 2011 by the University of Iowa Press
www.uiowapress.org
Printed in the United States of America
Text design by Richard Hendel

The University of Iowa Press is a member of Green
Press Initiative and is committed to preserving natural
resources.
Printed on acid-free paper

Library of Congress Cataloging-in-Publication Data
Alvarado, Beth.
Anthropologies : a family memoir / Beth Alvarado.—
1st ed.
    p.   cm.—(Sightline books, the Iowa series in
literary nonfiction)
Includes bibliographical references.
ISBN-13: 978-1-60938-037-3 (pbk)
ISBN-10: 1-60938-037-1 (pbk)
ISBN-13: 978-1-60938-038-0 (e-bk)
ISBN-10: 1-60938-038-X (e-bk)
    1. Authors, American—21st century—Biography.
I. Alvarado, Beth.   II. Alvarado, Beth—Family.
III. Alvarado, Beth—Homes and haunts.   IV. Alvarado,
Beth—Marriage.   V. Title.   VI. Title: Family memoir.
PS3601.L864Z46 2011   2011008423
813'.6—dc22

IN MEMORY OF

MARGARET JONES TAYLOR CORYELL

AND MARÍA DORA ROMERO ALVARADO

AND THE STORIES THEY BOTH TOLD.

Is it not possible — I often wonder — that things we have felt with great intensity have an existence independent from our minds; are in fact still in existence?

—VIRGINIA WOOLF, *Moments of Being*

Contents

Part One. Notes on Silence

It is also true that memory sometimes comes to him as a voice. It is a voice that speaks inside him, and it is not necessarily his own.
—Paul Auster, *The Invention of Solitude*

My mother and I are sitting in the small dining room of her town-house; we are sitting at the table she's had since I was a girl, but I am nearly fifty. The table is warm in the sunlight, the wood a dark grain; she'd found it in an old junk shop and asked the man to refinish it, the same junk shop where she'd found her baby grand piano, also in pieces, also in need of repair and refinishing. Now the piano sits in the living room beneath large triangular windows that, if you were ever to open the curtains, look out on the tee of a golf course. She no longer plays golf. She no longer plays the piano. She no longer paints Chinese watercolors or plays bridge with her friends. Most weeks I am the only one who visits, most nights, the only one who calls. She must be lonely, I think, but she says she isn't. With her halo of white hair, she is still beautiful. It's her brown eyes, maybe, her bone structure, the classical symmetry of her features. The oxygen machine hums in the background. The small interior courtyard behind her is full of light and green plants, most of them silk. She picks up crumbs of toast from the table with her finger and dusts them on to her plate.

She wants to tell me her stories, and every time I come to bring her groceries or make her soup or take her to see a doctor, she revises them. She has to get them just right. She wants me—she wants *some-one*, it doesn't have to be me, it's only by chance that I am the one child left in town to care for her—she wants someone to know her before she dies. This is my theory. When we were young, she never told these stories. Even ten years ago, she wasn't ready. My brother would ask, when he visited, to hear about his father. Oh, she'd say, getting up from the table, what is there to tell? We were married for so short a time. Only five years.

On Wednesdays and Sundays I type her stories into my laptop. It takes her a while, sometimes, to get started. I have to prompt her. Tell me the one about the dinner party, when Scottie pretended he was a waiter and gave your bill to the Navy guys. She laughs, remembering, maybe, the dress she was wearing that night, cream-colored with fuchsia and dark green designs, shoulder pads, the silky fabric knotted between her breasts. She shakes her head. When she tried to flick her cigarette butt out over the balcony, it hit Scottie's commanding officer in the forehead. What a faux pas! But she is amused by this younger self, I can tell. The oxygen machine makes little puffing sounds. I change it to the other setting. Her color is not so good today, she seems out of breath, and so I read to her something she dictated the time before. Oh, she says, just say, "my sister." Don't put her name. Don't put Dorothy. Or, oh, we can't say the officer's name. It might be a military secret. *His name?* You know, that he was there, on Saipan. Before Korea. When I give her the drafts for her approval, she draws thick black lines through certain phrases and details. Her life looks like a communiqué from the front or from prison.

2

My mother is holding her hand out, palm up. Her hand is empty—I am eighteen and she's trying to convince me to go to Europe—but in it, I see coins. Pennies. We are standing in the living room with the blue carpet and the cream-colored drapes. Behind me, the baby grand piano; behind her, the gilded mirror. My mother is smaller than I am. Her hair is in a French twist. She is wearing a smart pantsuit. In the kitchen my father is splashing coke over whiskey and ice cubes in a tall glass. My mother is telling me that once, when she was younger than me, maybe fourteen, her mother tried to give her pennies. They were all she had and my mother had refused them. She had knocked them out of her mother's hand and they had spun across the wooden floor, clinked into the furnace grate. This is the lesson of the story: how sharper than a serpent's tooth it is to *be* a thankless child.

But I have a stony heart. I'm eighteen. I have a boyfriend named Walker who doesn't want me to leave him, and even though I *want* to leave him, the thought of hearing him go on and on about it makes me tired. I will give in to almost anything for a little silence. This is how I am, a very old, a very tired eighteen. There are marks on my arms, but my mother has never mentioned them. There is a distance between us. You have built a wall around yourself—she says this sometimes—and I can't get in. But I am thinking, you don't want in. You don't want to hear the truth. You just want me to be someone else.

I am standing before her, a skinny eighteen-year-old girl, long hair, black tee shirt, baggy bell bottoms. It is 1972. I have marks on my arms and a stony heart. *What*, she is thinking, *what do you want from me?* She holds out her empty hand. She believes in gestures, not words. She believes in the liftoff of the jet, in crossing the ocean, in being incommunicado, in clearing your mind.

3

A swimming pool in the backyard, blue and unwavering. My father drinks too much whiskey. My mother's heels click across the cold tile floors, telegraphing her displeasure. They orbit silently around one another in the brick house at the end of a cul-de-sac. Double doors open onto a white marble foyer, living room with pale blue carpeting to the left, formal dining room to the right. Pale blue figures dance the minuet across the walls. Carriages are forever waiting.

There was something to fear in that house. Ghosts. Silence. Secrets kept. *What haunts are not the dead but the gaps left within us by the secrets of others.* Once, feverish with pneumonia, I left my body and floated down the long hallway. Past my parents' room, past the bathroom, past my sister's. All empty. I had come loose in time. No one else was home: the kitchen, empty, counters clean, mail stacked neatly on the island, grocery list, tomatoes, bread crossed out, milk; my father's office, no one, sheets of paper littered across the top of his desk, maps rolled up. The family room, TV off, the pool dark water on the other side of the glass doors, glass like pools of black, and it's night, late, late, and my little sister and I hear piano music coming from the living room, faint music like a song heard through a window on a summer night. We both hear it, think it must be our mother, the song so like a melody she used to sing when we were small. We get up, walk into the living room and there is no one, the music has stopped. My sister, frightened, disappears, but I am still loose in time. I touch the baby grand my mother refinished, run my hand on the smooth wood, prop open the lid, the strings like a harp. Sit down, place my hands on the worn keys, yellowed ivory. My fingers can still span one note more than an octave. The sheet music translates into recital pieces my fingers remember as if nothing passes through consciousness. Für Elise, The Spinning Song, the others I taught myself, Theme from a Summer Place. My mother's music so complicated I can't even read it. Another book, What Child Is This, O Holy Night, songs I play for my father, the light on the piano reflecting off the music, my father somewhere outside that circle of light on the dark sofa, listening. Even though I cannot see him, I know his head is cocked to one side, he is lost in thought. Sometimes my fingers fumble or the song ends and he is startled, clears his throat, then mumbles assent, appreciation. This is enough for me to keep playing.

My father. He is so preoccupied. Every time I want to talk to him, a little voice in my head—my mother's?—always asks, does this matter? Does this really matter? Is this important enough to disturb your father? Once he is present, he is fully present, passionate even. When I tell him that one of my friends has died from a heroin overdose, the sob of grief that escapes him is so primal it frightens me. He tells me, "I love you. I love you more than life itself." And I believe him. I imagine that he is willing to die for me, but I can also see that passion is dangerous. When you feel as deeply as my father does, you are vulnerable, too vulnerable; you must keep yourself safely wrapped in a cocoon of work or alcohol; you need relief, some way of distancing yourself from the world.

It seems to me, then, that everything important lies beneath the surface, in a pool of dark silence. My mother's sorrows and her fears, my father's passions, all unspoken. This kind of silence makes everything in waking life seem unreal. Or surreal. It disconnects the outside from the inside, you from your feelings, the present moment from memory. What matters is hidden away but, in being hidden, takes on power.

In my nightmare, a man waits in the corner of the living room; he grabs my arm when I round the corner to play the piano. He is the same man who, in dreams, pops up from the backseat of my car, and each time, although I am startled awake, it takes forever for the image of his eyes looking into mine to fade. Sometimes as I play the piano, I expect to feel his ghost breath next to my ear. But maybe he isn't a ghost, maybe he's a metaphor; maybe he isn't evil but represents, instead, the indifference of the universe, the wrenching of sudden loss. How loss might feel like evil, like someone's ill wishes, delivered.

4

There is a picture of my mother, taken when she is thirteen, her head slanted coyly, this look in her eyes like wonder. She is twenty-three when she meets her first husband, Scott. He calls her "the girl with the legs." He wants a date with the girl with the legs. In the pictures, he is always in uniform, a Marine. Hat tilted over one eye, almost rakish. She is Ingrid Bergman beautiful. She follows him everywhere. Boston, Camp Pendleton, Bremerton, Kansas, Saipan — by then they have two children — Oahu and back to Camp Pendleton. In the middle of the night, she will wake up and know Scott has been killed. A bullet has entered the right hip and made its way up through major organs and exited through the left shoulder. They are under heavy fire. They cannot evacuate him until morning. In the middle of the night, she hears his voice saying, I will always take care of you. *South Pacific* will always make her cry. Puccini, *Madama Butterfly*, is exquisite pain. Everything that heals also cuts.

All sorrows, Isak Dinesen writes, can be borne if you put them in a story, but my mother never talked about Scott. She didn't tell me about him until I was eight years old. We mustn't talk about him, she said, it hurts your father's feelings, and she never did. She never talked about him at the dinner table. She must have thought about him. Must have missed him. Must have seen him in my older sister and brother. But she never said anything about him, not even something as simple or as casual as, your father always held his fork like that.

You have his knack for drawing.

The Lord's Prayer and the Twenty-third Psalm, The Lord is my Shepherd, I shall not want. Beautiful copies of medieval manuscripts sent to me by my godmother when I am fourteen, beautiful red and blue lettering, the music of King James, gold scroll I trace with my finger. But my mother rolls them up and puts them in the top of the closet. I do not want to see these every time I enter your room. I've been to too many funerals, she says, they always say these at funerals.

There was something fragile in my mother, something that made me want to protect her. Even when I was very young, I knew she was afraid, afraid of loss. Her life had been defined by loss. *I shall not want.* I imagined her saying this every night as she fell asleep, every day as she walked around the house. I shall not want, I shall not want, I shall not want.

5

The window above the kitchen sink is fogged from hot steam. I am waiting to rinse. With my closed fist, I make a footprint, and then little points for the toes. What is outside? Beyond the steam? Snow. An edge of snow along the top of the wooden fence, a blanket of snow with paw prints and footprints bitten into the thin crust on top. Ice on the flagstone porch makes it a shiny red. In a month under the eaves crocuses will begin to poke through. First the spears of their leaves and then, shyly, the white globe of the flower.

This memory takes place in Grand Junction, when I am a child. Before we've moved to Tucson and the house with the swimming pool. Before 1968, the year that marks the end of my childhood. 1968. When we cross that line, the one dividing Colorado from Arizona, we leave my brother and sister behind, my two small nieces. At night, my heart aches for them. We cross the state line and enter a landscape full of cacti and orange trees, a land of perpetual summer. My parents' marriage begins to disintegrate or perhaps I simply begin to notice. I smoke pilfered cigarettes in the shower in the mornings. There is a window. I crank it open. I wonder what would happen if someone, a boy from school, say, were to walk by.

But go back to winter, back to Grand Junction. I am a child. My mother hands me a plate slick with soapy water. *She* is in Hayward this morning, in her own childhood, in the large Victorian house where she grew up. It was the Depression. She was the youngest of nine, born when her own mother was forty-five years old. The house was white, two stories, cupolas, an attic, a widow's walk, everything! A fireplace in every room. A long winding staircase. At Christmas, open the parlor doors and there is the tree. It touches the ceiling; there is a lit candle on every branch. My grandfather, the story is, won the house in a poker game. The people who had lived there, from England, disappeared, leaving behind all of the heavy ornate furniture and Oriental rugs, their books in the library, the china and silver, even the portraits of their grandfathers, stern men with long beards. When you crossed the parlor, my mother always said, their eyes followed you.

Their eyes followed you, but they weren't our ancestors, those British patriarchs. Our ancestors were Mormons who crossed the country with Brigham Young. When Elizabeth, my great-great-grandmother, was just a girl, they sent for her to scrub Joseph Smith's blood out of the cobblestones of the Carthage Jail. When she was still in her teens, she married a married man, a poor cobbler, and they went west. When I am in my twenties, my mother will give me a copy of her story typed on yellowing paper; she had dictated it to her daughter and, decades later, it was collected by the WPA. In it, Elizabeth says she will "end now as someone else has to do my writing for me." Her voice, I think this must be her voice: the mobs howled around Nauvoo, herds of buffalo sounded like thunder, the dust raised from their hooves covered the sun. The prairie, the desolate prairie. After they left Winter Quarters, her baby girl died and she had to leave her behind on the desolate prairie. West, she said, she followed her husband west, to Bountiful where the desert bloomed, and then to Sacramento where the other wives and her husband died, where the floods came and rattlesnakes were as thick as a man's arm and she shot a cougar out of a tree just before it pounced on her son. Sacramento, where she finished raising their twenty children by herself. She will stop now, she says, as someone else has to do her writing for her; she will stop with this small postscript about raising twenty children.

In the story my mother tells about her, she is in the last wagon of the train and a small band of Indians rides up and she doesn't know if they're friendly or not and so she shows them the baby and asks them, *savez-vous* smallpox? And the Indians gallop away. But it isn't until years later that I'll wonder about this story, about why Elizabeth hadn't included it in her own telling. Is it someone else's story, then? Maybe one that has come down through time, in family after family, a kind of old-fashioned urban legend about how the west was won? One of her daughters, another Elizabeth, my mother's grandmother, became the store-bought bride of a Welshman and so the Mormon branch withers, becomes Episcopalian. My mother remembers her grandmother as a taciturn woman who sat in a rocker on the porch day after summer day. She never spoke. She rarely turned her head. She was so old, so old her earlobes nearly reached her shoulders because, as you know, my mother says, the ears keep growing while the head does not.

All stories circle back to Hayward, back to my mother's childhood where handsome is as handsome does and blood is thicker than water and you reap what you sow. My mother said these things and she believed them, that such symmetry was possible. Back to Hayward, where everything was pastoral: carpets of iris in the spring, white jasmine trailing over the windows, their vines casting shadows on the walls in the hallway. White lace curtains. Her oldest sister, Dorothy, stood on the landing during a full moon, scent of jasmine wafting in the window, and recited "The Highwayman." In the daytime, while their mother canned peaches in the kitchen below, my mother hid in the attic and read, looked out at the garden, at the fig trees and forsythia, the roses and wisteria. There were treasures in the attic: an ostrich egg, an elephant tusk, smooth ivory, a bottle of water from the River Jordan, cool against her cheek. My mother and her sister Elizabeth jumped from the barn roof with umbrellas, hoping for flight.

Her father was a tall handsome man, a few years younger than her mother. Her mother, tiny, black eyes, deep dimples in her cheeks, was smitten. He drove a horse and buggy when he courted her. Picked her up from the schoolhouse and took her into town. He was a rancher, a sheriff, a stockbroker until the market collapsed. He chewed raw garlic for his heart and drank cold buttermilk with a pinch of salt in the summer. Brought chicken tamales home from the city, the spicy tender meat wrapped in layers and layers of whispery corn husks tied with string at each end. He threatened the Chinaman who did his laundry: too much starch and he would cut off his pigtail. My mother always laughed, almost wistfully, as she told us what this meant, that the Chinaman could not get into Heaven without his pigtail, that therefore her father was a clever man, a powerful man, more clever even than those clever Chinese, those inscrutable Chinese.

I've seen a picture of my grandfather in uniform. The Spanish American War. Riding pants, a cavalry hat, his large dark moustache. He had such a presence, my mother always marveled, when he walked into a restaurant, people noticed. When he came home from the city, he would sit in a white wicker chair under the shade trees and I would sit on his knee and put my arm around his neck. I would kiss his cheek even though he smelled like garlic. I would take tiny sips of his buttermilk.

6

How I hated him, Aunt Dorothy says. She is lying on a bed in assisted living, her long white hair falling across her pillow, her pale blue eyes, her hands knotted in front of her. Because she rarely gets out of bed, my mother and I turn it so that it faces the window, but she lies there most days with her eyes closed and what she sees, I cannot see. Morphine dreams or perhaps dreams from eating so little, end-of-life dreams. When I hold the glass with water, the straw to her lips, her chin trembles as she drinks. In the square of the second-story window, a palm tree, the nest of a dove in the tiny vee where the frond meets the trunk. The dove, gray with darker markings on her neck and wing, watches us with one eye.

In the city, my grandfather had a mistress for thirty-five years. (My mother never told me this story. This is Aunt Dorothy's story, Dorothy, the oldest daughter, Dorothy, who took care of my mother after their mother died.) When my grandmother found out—someone had mistakenly sent her the dry cleaning bill for the other woman's drapes—she climbed the stairs to her bedroom and had her first stroke. My grandfather waited by her side all night. Their son, the doctor, lived nearby, but my grandfather didn't call him. She turned blue. He was waiting for her to die. By morning, she had turned black but was still alive, and so he knocked on Dorothy's bedroom door and said, your mother is ill. She needs you.

My aunt's eyes are closed. She is so tired. Her dead husband comes to her in dreams or perhaps they are visions, but she says she is not ready to follow him. I never told your mother, she tells me, she loved Father so much. Adored him. But which was worse? To shatter her innocence? Or to allow her to believe a lie? And now I see, I see the house in Hayward as the place where silence starts, a place where things happened that everyone wants to forget. You could write a novel about it—my aunt Dorothy sighs—it would be an American tragedy.

7

Some mornings, my mother is in the apartment in the Haight-Ashbury district where her father moved them after he sold the house in Hayward. She is a voice student at San Francisco State. From the window of their apartment, she can look down on the school. The voices and sounds of instruments, scales on the piano, violins being tuned, float up. There is a dirt courtyard in the middle of the wooden buildings. The choir has been chosen to sing with the San Francisco Opera, Wagner, the harsh German words transformed by music; the girl next to her has too much vibrato in her voice and my mother is afraid the conductor will think it is her. Months later, she will audition for a part in the San Francisco Opera, she is a slight figure on stage in front of an empty auditorium; there is only one man way at the back, listening. He tells her to go home and sing for her mother. And so she does—at least this is how she tells the story—she gives up music, she goes home and takes care of her mother as she dies, stroke by stroke. My mother, the youngest of nine, the only one left now that her father has gone to live with his mistress. My mother at eighteen, brushing her mother's hair. Sometimes her mother looks at her and doesn't recognize her. Sometimes she sits for hours in her wheelchair before the window. She doesn't speak. She doesn't say, Margaret, bring me some tea. She doesn't say, read to me.

8

Margaret flies on a seaplane filled with Marines to Saipan. It is 1946. Her husband, Scott, is already there. She has with her her dark-haired daughter, one year old and barely walking. She has been told to pack into trunks everything they will need for two years: clothing, diapers, dishes, linens. She is seven months pregnant. There are no seats in the plane, only slings on which the soldiers sit. How long is the flight? Hours. From evening to morning. The pilots joke about the engines going out. The ocean is far below, dark and cold and probably choppy. The attending doctor gives her his bunk so that she and her daughter can sleep. They fly all night and then in the morning stop in Hawaii where they have to wait until the next day for an even smaller plane to take them to Saipan. In Hawaii, they stay in the Royal Hawaiian where they have a room overlooking the gardens and beach. The next evening, while the sun is still shining, she and her little daughter will lean out the window of their room and see on the lawn below them the "Royal Hawaiians" playing their ukuleles and guitars. Hula girls dance in their grass skirts, their hands singing a story.

On Saipan, Scottie has painted the floors of the Quonset hut with creosote to keep the bugs out, but it smells and is sticky. It is so hot that Margaret lets the shower run all day so that she and Marilyn can walk in and out to cool themselves off. The Quonset hut looks out on a lagoon, the water body-temperature and pale green, then a coral reef. The maid catches fish for her dinner there. The neighbor, with her glass-bottomed box, swims all day watching, below her, the exotic fish. In the evening, she makes drinks with lemon and rum and sugar. They're called bees' knees and she and Margaret sit and watch the children play in the sand and drink bees' knees and smoke cigarettes, flicking them out, away, the red embers glowing like the sinking sun. This is after World War II but before Korea. Japanese soldiers are still hiding in caves up in the hills. They don't know the war is over.

Footsteps, first one and then a long silence and then another. Scottie is on night duty. Margaret is alone with the children. She crawls out of bed, takes the service revolver out of the dresser drawer, loads it. Her children are babies, asleep on the bed, and so she sits on the edge of the bed, facing the doorway. She sits there all night, the gun getting heavier and heavier, sweat dripping off her face. The footsteps, she can hear them and, in between, it is quiet, so quiet she can hear the jungle growing. Then the light. Birds. Morning sounds, the children waking, and she realizes, only then does she realize what she's been hearing. Banana slugs. Squishy, yellow banana slugs, as they dropped from the papaya trees onto the tin roof of the Quonset hut.

9

Scott borrows a jeep and they drive, with the children, top down, to the top of the green island. The ocean, from there, a blue blue beyond, á la *South Pacific*. They visit the outcrop at one end of the island where the Japanese jumped to their deaths rather than be captured. They walk the rest of the mountain, looking into foxholes, posing for pictures. There are bombs, unexploded. Margaret is carrying the baby, three or four months old, and they fall into a foxhole. There is nothing in it but long grass, a blue chink of sky above, a single cloud, then Scottie, laughing as he reaches down for the baby, as he reaches down to help her out. His face is in shadow but she knows his eyes are blue, there is a deep cleft in his chin, a cleft that will be repeated in his son's chin and in his granddaughter's twenty years later and, then, in her son's. But today he is twenty-seven and carefree, invincible. A wind comes up. They climb into the jeep. She laughs. There is not yet, inside of her, a hard seed between the heart and rib cage.

10

My father, at fifteen, rows around and around Vashon Island, delivering groceries, the wind in his face, the waves washing against the boat. The island rises out of Puget Sound behind him, the small white house tucked up against a forest primeval, the narrow pebbled beach piled high with driftwood, logs burned white by the salt of the ocean. He looks off toward the mainland, toward Mount Rainier in the distance. As he pulls the boat through water, he feels each muscle clearly delineated, in his arms, his shoulders, his back. Annapolis at sixteen, an officer in the war, his sweet young face in the photographs. When his mother stood on the shore, she could see him out there; she lifted her voice against the wind but he couldn't hear her.

My father meets my mother when he picks her up for a bridge game. As she bounds down the steps of the house where she lives with her two small children, it is as if he has seen the photograph of her at thirteen, the innocence and mischief in her eyes. As if he can see the future, my birth and the birth of my younger sister, two children he never thought he would have. My mother slides into the car seat next to him, her dark hair curls to her shoulders, her red lips, white teeth, delicate wrists: a life opens up before him.

II

My father was a solitary man, even when we were young, in the family house, a solitary man but not necessarily a lonely one. His silence was the silence of a scientist, of a man preoccupied with large and weighty concerns. When he wasn't out in the field, he was enclosed in a small room surrounded by maps and boxes of data. He lived in some other era — Precambrian, perhaps, or Mesozoic — and thought in terms of vast stretches of time. Humankind must have seemed to him a blip on the screen; human drama, or even human tragedy, a distraction in the larger scheme of things. I remember watching his face. Whenever I came to him with a problem or even a simple question, he had to wrench himself into the present moment. He wasn't of the 20th century. When he met someone, he gave a little bow in deference. He always thought in terms of honor — so and so was an honorable man or not an honorable man — and this mattered to him, this, above all. Better to give someone the benefit of the doubt, he'd say, even if later they prove you wrong.

My father was a solitary man, not necessarily a lonely one. And yet, and yet, the long phone messages he left on my mother's answering machine after their divorce when I was thirty-four. His sigh as he would tell me he was waiting to buy a house she would like; if he ever bought a house again, he wanted her to help him pick it out. This, even though she would never answer his messages. (And this: she never erased them from the machine; the sound of his voice, after he died, she gave to me.) The narrow path through his apartment, from dining area, through the living room, into the bedroom, a narrow path, towers of boxes on either side, the couch stacked with boxes of files, rolls of maps everywhere. Stacks of old newspapers. Geology journals. It was as if his research had rented the apartment, and he merely sublet: cooked in the kitchen, sat at the table, slept in the bed. Was he lonely? When my sister and I cleaned out his apartment, I kept sighing, *Oh, Daddy*, and so maybe I did think he was lonely, maybe I did think there was something sad, something not chosen about his life. Oh, Daddy. *Stop that*, my sister said, *stop sighing, stop saying that*. Because she had always seen what I was just beginning to see? His regret, his mistakes. His distance from all of us.

12

At the Palace of Fruits on a summer evening, I wear red socks in
my white sandals, my father carries a watermelon under his arm, my
mother holds up boxes of sparklers, gold, red, blue, for my little sister
and me to see. She takes a rubber band off her wrist and pulls her hair
up into a ponytail. In the evenings, he comes home from work and
pours bourbon into a tall glass over ice, she stretches up on her toes
and puts her arms around his neck. His pant legs are gray and baggy.
Her feet are bare. They kiss. The evening light slants across the tablecloth with the little yellow flowers.

13

The landscape of my childhood is tree-lined and green, the Bookcliffs jutting barren from sandy earth, the canals they drag for the bodies of lost swimmers, the irrigation flume where you should never go. The old white, three-story house in the middle of the alfalfa field. Upstairs the bathtub has claw feet. Upstairs my older sister's friend lies in bed with typhus. Will her hair fall out? This is what we wonder as we push each other higher and higher on the rope swing under the cottonwoods.

I sometimes long to go back to childhood, to winter, to shadow-blue ski trails as they wind through the trees, back to the slicing sound of my skis on ice crystals. Back to aspens, their leaves like shimmering gold coins, aspens bare and stark, the horizon behind them as blue and cold as water. Back, even, to snow banked gray and dirty against winter curbs, the slow dripping of icicles from the eaves, the air outside the bed as cold as a knife, dark sky, stars so far away you think about your mother dying. That's what stars do when you are little, they make you think about light lost in the universe, about time, about your younger sister, asleep beside you. She was small then and the only one you loved fiercely.

14

Your sister was small, then, a baby, and your mother took her into a small white cabin. She said, don't disturb us. We are going to take a nap. She shut the screen door. She shut the door behind it. It was summer. Afternoon. There was a lake. Where was your father? Was he prospecting? There was gravel on the ground. There were trees behind the cabin. It was hot and smelled of sun on pine needles. There was a lake. Your older sister and brother put you in the rowboat and then they climbed in. Your brother rowed. He rowed you out to the diving platform floating offshore. It was square, made of gray wooden planks. Then you and your sister were on the platform and your brother was rowing away. Did you have your swimming suits on? Were you going swimming? You dangled your feet in the water. Your sister and brother were arguing. He was rowing around and around the platform. There were white cabins on the shore, their windows shut against daylight. In one of them, your mother was asleep with your baby sister. You were not to disturb her. How old were you? Four? Your older sister? Twelve? The clouds were rising behind the trees now and a big shadow fell across the lake. The horseflies came out. They started biting. They were big with big gray wings, they had red spots on their heads. It was a long way to shore. There was thunder. The water got gray and choppy. Maybe you started crying. Maybe your sister yelled so loud that your brother finally rowed back to get you. You don't remember that part, you remember only the gravel beneath your bare feet, the horseflies, the welts on your arms and thighs, and then you remember banging and banging and banging on the white wooden frame of the screen door.

15

My mother is playing the piano, Rachmaninoff, she loved the Russians, the difficulty of the phrasing. I sit on the bench beside her. She stops and looks at me. My mouth opens but there it is, the image as if from on high: a version of myself standing in the trailer behind the neighbor's house. I am six years old and I am standing naked and the girl, my friend, is naked, and her older cousin, a teenager, is sitting there. He wants us to touch the hill under his pants and Hilary does. She reaches out one finger and she touches it. A flash of heat and yellow. Exit the body. Exit the trailer, the screen door slapping closed behind me. Hilary's mother, her face in the kitchen window. Am I naked? Am I clutching before me the beach towel or the bathing suit? Or have I dressed myself? I try to remember. My mother has paused. She is patient. My mouth opens and closes. She says something about a man in the Bible who complains about having no shoes until he meets a man who has no feet. This is meant to comfort me. She begins to play again. Rachmaninoff.

Out the front window, the begonias are a waxy red. Dig a fingernail into the thick fleshy leaf, leave a crescent moon, a mark so you can remember, a mark because memory is the continuous present, because memory is a room. If you mark it, you will be able to enter again, you will be able to see the light, the people, what they are doing, what they are wearing. Their mouths will move. But what is it they are saying? If you are very still, if you don't breathe, maybe you will be able to hear the words. What did Hilary say? What did her cousin say? And you, what did you tell your mother?

Memory is a silent room, a home movie from an old Brownie camera. A woman places a cake with candles on a picnic table. A man waterskis. A girl is wearing a pink leotard. She is tap dancing on the front porch near the begonias. Her empty hand, which one assumes will hold a black top hat on the night of the performance, tips the invisible hat on top of her head and then holds it in front of her chest, then tips it on her head again, then back in front of the chest. The look on her face is one of concentration. She is not smiling but neither is she unhappy. Then the younger sister, round and dimpled, dressed in fluffy white, hair in pigtails. She is delighted. She wears white gloves and at the end, she curtsies, blows kisses. She is a young girl doing a tap dance for her mother's camera. Remember the ticking of the film? The way it melts across the screen when it's over?

16

My older sister drives a turquoise '56 Chevy, an old boxy car for 1963, not sleek, no fins. Some evenings she puts my little sister and me in the backseat. We pick up her friend. They both have their hair rolled up on orange juice cans, scarves thrown over. They hold cigarettes gingerly and little puffs of smoke come out of their mouths. Wolfman Jack on the radio. My little sister and I are to duck when cute boys pull up next to our car at the red light. We cruise Orchard Avenue between the Top Hat and the Arctic Circle.

Grand Junction in the early 60s, no one locks doors at night. Teenagers walk on dark streets to Lincoln Park. Their mothers never have to warn them. There is no crime. We ride our bikes up and down the leafy avenues all night long. Listen to crickets through the open windows as we fall asleep. Spend hours lying on the lawn watching clouds. In spring, the fragrant tumble of lilac blossoms; pansies and violets have sweet faces. In summer, begonias spill out of the planter; sunny marigolds edge the lawn below. My father has planted Russian olive trees all around the house, in threes, hollowed out rooms inside the hedge for my younger sister and me. From our secret hideout, we spy on our big brother as he and his friends work on an old jalopy, and on our older sister when the forbidden brown-skinned boy drops her off after school. He has his arm around her, he kisses her, we see them, parked right there, at the end of the long driveway under the birches.

When we walk by the public pool where we are not allowed to swim because of polio and where everyone else in town swims, my mother says that blacks and Mexicans don't get along because no one likes to be at the bottom. My father says that other people are just different. When he was in Mexico, once, there was a funeral for a child and everyone was crying, but they still let their children ride in the backs of the trucks. They don't value life the same way we do, he says. Like the Indians, he says, shaking his head, and I remember that one time, on the way to Salt Lake City, it had been raining, it was a very bad accident. My father had helped lift the truck off the body of a small girl. I remembered. I remembered how upset he was, throwing up by the car afterwards. But I also remembered the time I saw a body of a man by the side of the road. We were going to a restaurant. It was winter, it was dark and still snowing. And I told my father and he said to the manager, there is a man lying a mile or so back, next to the highway. The manager handed us the menus. Oh, he said, it's probably just a drunk Indian. That's how people talked then. Wop, mick, spic, jungle bunny. Drunk Indian. But my father went to the pay phone anyway and called the police.

At the country club, where we are allowed to swim, our brother does back dives and cannonballs. I like the cool water, the dim green world where my little sister and I swim toward each other, tiny bubbles in our hair as we float face to face, our hair like dark seaweed. Larger bubbles rise, round as vowels, when we speak. They capture light in water.

17

We love the belly of the ferry where we park the car, the echoing stairway up to the deck, the cold air and wind in our faces. Our eyes tear. Gulls follow us, the whir of their wings, their raucous calling for popcorn. The island rises before us. The boat creaks and thuds against dark pilings. At the last minute, we race back to the car. In the forest, on the narrow road up to the point, my father honks before we round each curve. Then down the long path we walk, down through the rainforest, trees like a dark tunnel, my older sister holding my hand. There is a white rail where the hillside fell away. Far below, we see patches of roofs, smoke curling from chimneys, the glinting gray light of Puget Sound. We climb the crooked stairs down to our grandparents' house.

This is the summer house, where my father and his brothers spent their childhoods learning how to play tennis on the clay court, where they picked blackberries and delivered groceries during the Depression, had picnics and bonfires on the beach with all the neighbors, made bows and arrows from alder trees, took piano and dance lessons. Dance lessons. Although he will sometimes put Benny Goodman on the record player and try to teach me how to fox-trot, I cannot imagine my father in dance lessons. In leotards. I'm told they wore leotards! In the pictures of their childhood, he and his three brothers wear short pants, velvet breeches, their hair in golden waves. During the school year, they lived in town, in Seattle, in the family home on Green Lake. During the Depression, my grandfather, a lawyer, often walked home from the office so that he could give his fare to someone who needed it for food. This is what my father tells me, that it is important to be generous, and it is true of my grandfather. Years later, at his funeral, people we don't know will speak of his small acts of kindness.

In ten years, when I am sixteen, my grandfather, pale blue eyes, a hawk nose like Charles DeGaulle's, will begin to live in the past: my father will become his best friend, the guy who helped him grease the trolley tracks so they could watch the cars slide backwards down the Seattle hills. I will become his sister who died years before. Matchsticks will become car keys, words will elude him. But for now, he teaches me to build a fire in the fireplace: first the kindling, then the twigs and sticks in a tent, then the larger pieces of wood. At low tide, my father rolls his trousers up and shows us where to dig for clams. We put them in a bucket of seawater on the back porch and wait for their rubbery necks to stretch out. In the morning, my mother wakes us early to pick blackberries for breakfast. In the afternoons, my grandmother bakes sugar cookies with tiny threads of lemon peel.

18

The house on Green Lake, when we stand on the sidewalk below, towers over us. It is three stories tall and it is two stories of stairs up from the sidewalk to reach it. We stand dwarfed by the house of my father's childhood. We try to imagine him sleeping in one of the bedrooms upstairs, no heat at night, not even in winter, we're told, windows open. This was good, they believed, for the constitution. This large Victorian house, dark wood, built by our great-grandfather in the 1880s, was one of the first on the block. Back then, from the porch, from the wide front windows, you could see Green Lake, the park, the dark woods beyond. My grandfather had grown up in this house, and when he and my grandmother moved in with their two oldest boys, it must have seemed a dream to her, to live in such a house, a house with a terraced flower garden. Here is where she threw parties and held dances during the war. She even invited a fiddler, and the soldiers on leave and the USO girls or the girls from church would come and everyone would dance and afterwards my grandmother would let the soldiers sleep in beds in the basement and maybe, even, upstairs in the boys' beds because three of her four sons were in the service and so their beds were empty. KennyGeorgeKirbyDon. She said their names as if they were one name. What would she have done if the chain were broken? Did she ever allow herself to wonder? As we stand below on the sidewalk, we imagine the large front room, a parlor, we guess, furniture pushed back to the edges, wood floors gleaming. We imagine the fiddlers, the dance, and then the breathless dancers as they spill outside onto the front porch and into the night air.

19

In the old photographs of my grandfather's family home in upstate New York, the women wear long black dresses with bustles. They sit in chairs on the front porch and do needlepoint. Tatting. They write poems in one another's autograph albums, the pages now yellowed, some of the handwriting so faded—*Ever beauteous be thy dreams*—that it's difficult to read. 1854. June 1854. Montgomery. Oswego. One hundred years before my birth. *Dearest Libby, Better to trust and be deceived / And weep that trust and that deceiving*—my grandmother gives me the autograph book because my name is Elizabeth. Elizabeths from both sides of the family converge in me—I am the only sibling to have a family name—but rather than making me feel as if my self goes back generations, it makes me feel as if I have no particular self, as if my mother couldn't think of a new name for me. Still, I get the autograph book, and that makes me happy, the red leather embossed in gold leaf: *Moss Rose Album*. A woman and an angel sit in a golden garden on the front. Inside, beautiful botanical drawings, in color, with tissue paper over them. It is, perhaps, worth sharing a name.

My grandmother is a tiny woman with bird-bright eyes. That house is now a library, she tells me, and this is coin silver. She shows me tablespoons, thin brittle silver, melted down from coins before the Revolutionary War, melted down so they wouldn't have to pay taxes to the King. These are your people, she seems to be saying, here before the Revolution, they fought on both sides, Whig and Tory. One of them owned Coryell's Ferry. Here, you see? It's where George Washington crossed the river. One of them was his pallbearer, a last-minute replacement, true, for someone else who came down with the flu, but still, she nods her head, this is where you come from, from Huguenots who fled France before the Revolutionary War. Emmanuel Coryell. It rhymes.

20

Freighters and tugboats set glassy waves rolling toward us. My little sister and I gather small stones and pieces of beach glass worn smooth, still tasting slightly of salt. Tiny tiny shells shaped like Chinese hats lie in the curled palm of her hand. We sit on driftwood, also worn smooth, trunks of trees worn nearly flat. The water laps gently, more like a lake than the ocean. It's hard to imagine winter, waves strong enough to wash these huge logs up on the shore. I have never been here in winter, only in summer, when the hydrangeas are in bloom and the blackberries ripe, when the sky is blue over the small white house, over the forest rising behind it, above the gray water.

Night is absolutely quiet. It hurts your ears. Pinpricks of stars, the lights of Seattle across the Sound, their reflection in water. And yet, it seems, everything unravels. My grandfather's mind. My parents' marriage. Even the landscape. In the middle of a rainy winter night, the house is pushed into the Sound by a mudslide; the Victorian loveseat, upholstered in maroon velvet, sits on the beach. There is a space in the air where the house used to be. The forest rises behind it. The tide churns small stones on the shore.

21

One day, it had been raining for so long. My grandmother and her younger brothers and sisters huddled on the bed in the living room while their mother tried to sweep the muddy water back out the front door. In the summers, they would row out to the island and camp. They were homesteading, walking off lots where they could build houses and grow crops. They cut their hair and tied it to stakes in the garden to keep the deer away.

Where do your people come from? This is a question my grandmother always asks. She, child of Scandinavian immigrants, whose mother took in sewing and whose father worked in a dry dock, grew up in a tiny house on a muddy street in Seattle just below where the Space Needle now stands. Her husband, my grandfather, came out from New York by train with his parents when he was a baby. They were from different circles, my grandparents. They were born Victorians, met and married in the new century. When she saw him in church, she understood the distance between them. He was the son of a lawyer who'd been the son of a doctor who'd been the son of a doctor, and so it went for generations. Her Bible is inscribed in a language other than English. These things mattered.

Now her spidery handwriting fills the gold-bound family Bible, the Bible of her husband's family. Her finger joints are fat with arthritis. Her eyes, although nearly blind, are bright with curiosity even when she's older than one hundred years, older than the automobile, the washing machine, the telephone, the TV, the airplane, satellites, and rocket ships.

In a speech he may or may not have given, Chief Seattle predicts that the spirits of Indians will walk up and down the hills, through the forests of Seattle and the islands of Puget Sound, long after they have died and the whites have come and built their houses. He does not believe in what Leslie Marmon Silko calls the spaghetti theory of history, the one where white people whip out a long noodle of time and say, "Things have changed,"—as in, "All injustices happened a long *long* time ago," as in, "Get over it."

No, Chief Seattle does not believe in linear time, he believes that all times coexist: here in this room with us are all the people who have ever been in this room. Time is a dimension, a place you might enter, and so it is with my grandmother. She has not gone backwards in time, does not live in the past as did my grandfather; instead time has come undone. When she tells stories about her past, they are stories that never happened to her. My mother, she would say, it was the greatest tragedy of my life, she died when I was eighteen. She would tell this story, over and over, day after day, and my father would say, every day, very patiently, Mother, your mother didn't die when you were eighteen. But maybe time is a dimension. Maybe my grandmother simply entered a room in another woman's past and it felt like home.

22

In the photograph of the summer house on Vashon, my grandparents are standing side by side on the front lawn. He is wearing dark slacks and a red checked flannel shirt and she, a flowered dress and blue cardigan. The house, which no longer stands, seems solid, permanent as the hillside that rises behind it and will someday obliterate it, but my grandparents, no longer alive, seem ephemeral, as if they are fading. There is no longer a line to distinguish the top of my grandfather's head from the white roof behind him; the crescents of his eyes and smile are all that's left of his face. My grandmother, too, her hair has merged with the siding of the house and the merest of shadows suggest her eyes, her nose, her mouth.

Part Two. Notes on Travel

*For if every true love affair can feel like a journey to a foreign
country, where you can't quite speak the language, and you don't
know where you're going, and you're pulled ever deeper into the
inviting darkness, every trip to a foreign country can be a love
affair, where you're left puzzling over who you are and whom
you've fallen in love with.*

—Pico Iyer, "Why We Travel"

I

At the restaurant, Fernando wipes a porthole clear with his sleeve. People on the boardwalk step into the clarity of the circle, just for an instant, and then back into the mist. Behind them, the gray sea-wall, the open ocean and sky, all gray, the surf pounding. It is raining, a misty rain. Sandpipers skirt the waves. A man with a beard stands gazing out at the ocean, then down at a small piece of paper he holds cupped in both hands. His lips move as if he were praying.

The room at the hotel is the same one we rented on our summer pilgrimages to San Diego, to water, when our children were young. Now they are grown and their absence momentarily astounds me. We leave the sliding-glass doors and curtains open for the cool breeze and the sound of waves. Fernando naps. I read *Love in the Time of Cholera*. Marquez. "The weak never enter the kingdom of love, which is a harsh and ungenerous kingdom." I put the book down and remember the woman on NPR who told of climbing into her husband's hospital bed as he lay dying of liver cancer. She put French music on the stereo because they never got to see Paris.

We have never been to Paris. We have never been to Italy. But we have raised two children. And this, Fernando believes, is what we were put on earth to do. He's actually said that to me: I have finished what I was put on earth to do. I don't quite understand it. I lie on my side, looking at the sea through the white bars of the balcony. I put my hand on his warm shoulder. No matter how long you have, there is never enough time. We wake up to a room flooded with sunlight.

Fireworks that night over the water. Our fingertips touch. Bursts of gaudy color cascade down to their reflections. My eyes love, especially, the silver ones: stars shooting out of a central blossom of color, purple, maybe, red. An electric blue. We plan our extravagant dinner. I will drink a crisp white wine. A grilled artichoke with aioli for starters. Then, for the gentleman, sea bass wrapped in a potato crust, tiny spring asparagus on the side. Lobster bisque for the lady? Grilled scallops on new greens? A lemon tart with crème fraiche for dessert. Two spoons. We will walk in the dark, our arms linked, all the way down to the roller-coaster. The edges of the waves, lit up by microscopic sea animals, glow an iridescent green. Is there a moon? We will make love with the sliding-glass doors open.

The last morning, the light on the ocean is slate blue, glassy, so beautiful it is painful to behold and I say, I see why you like to walk at this time. Then Fernando looks at me and in his eyes, that shy look of pleasure they have sometimes.

2

I am watching Fernando walk across the lawn near Old Main. There are huge olive trees on this side of campus, their dark limbs gnarled and low. This is in 1970 and I am staying in an old brick dorm with green linoleum on the floors. I have met Fernando before, but we will not start dating for a few years. He is tall. He has wavy hair. He is wearing jeans, cowboy boots, a white tee shirt. He saunters. His car, a muscle car, a red Plymouth Fury, is parked on the street behind him.

I am a student at the art camp where he works as a waiter. I am sitting on the grass watching him, writing a story. *Gravity is a serious thing—* (I write. I am sixteen.) *—it holds us here on earth, pulls us to her. Imagine gravity losing its hold. You will fly off. I will fly off. Everyone will fly off. Houses trees flowers barking dogs and freaked out cats. We'll all float into the air. Oranges from trees. Lemons. Spoons. Salt shakers. Cactus. The sky a blue soup full of random objects.* Without gravity, the fly could not settle on the napkin of the man in the poem the teacher had read that morning.

Can we have a fly in a poem? the writing teacher had asked. Can a chair be a work of art? the painting teacher had asked. In 1970, these were big questions. In California, Richard Brautigan wept. In Vietnam, boys I had not yet met smoked dope, injected heroin, slogged through the jungle and tried to stay alive. Here, in Tucson, I went to summer art classes. Here, on a street threading through campus, a Harley roared, and I imagined it taking flight.

The painting teacher had placed a kitchen chair, sanded wood, curved back, smooth wooden seat, in the center of the room. He had walked around it, considering it from all angles. An ordinary chair. What if Michelangelo had painted it, he asked. What if it were an ornate chair, carved for Louis the Sixteenth? Would we then consider it a work of art and not a chair? Perhaps he was the sculpture teacher. Perhaps we were supposed to consider objects from every angle, to look in our own backyards, to look back from a hundred years in the distance, to slide out of our skins and into the skin of someone else, someone with other eyes.

3

At the banquet, I am a guest, seated across from the deaf boy who writes poems full of unrequited love, missives left for years in rusting mailboxes. At the banquet, Fernando serves. He wears black slacks, a white long-sleeved shirt, a red vest. A monkey suit, he calls it. He is standing behind the deaf boy, mortified to see me or, perhaps, more accurately, to be seen by me. "It is," W. E. B. Dubois once said, "a peculiar sensation, this double consciousness, the sense of always looking at one's self through the eyes of others, of measuring one's soul by the tape of a world that looks on in amused contempt and pity."

Amused contempt and pity? That is what he thought. I will learn this later, years later, and yet at the time I had no class consciousness at all, no sense that my being the guest and his being the server had any significance, no sense that my being white and his being darker would matter to anyone other than my parents. I was simply happy to see him in the banquet hall full of artsy teenagers I did not know.

I give a little wave of greeting. He wants to disappear. The deaf boy cannot hear him ask if he wants a refill. Fernando stands there slightly behind him, pitcher sweating in his hand. I point to my ear surreptitiously, as if I am adjusting a strand of hair—I don't want the deaf boy to see and be offended—but Fernando will not look at me, will not meet my eyes, read my lips, or see my gestures.

In the kitchen, the server who is not allowed to serve—the black patch covers only the empty socket—has convinced Fernando not to join the Army. Ramon, although he is called Ray by the boss, arranges food on plates and plates on trays. He washes dishes. He had been a gunner on a boat in the Mekong Delta, and a round that did not explode but still shattered the shield took his eye, his cheekbone, the upper part of his eye socket. The black patch cannot cover the caved-in half of his face. The government will not cover cosmetic reconstruction.

I finally realize it is futile to gesture to a person who will not look at you, to say nothing to someone who is not deaf. *Fernando*, I say, *he can't hear you.* In English, "there is no one so blind as he who will not see" but in Spanish, "there is no one so deaf as he who will not listen." In Spanish, instead of throwing in the towel, one hangs up his tennies.

Our worlds are different, but not in the ways one might expect. As Fernando will point out often, he is *more* American than I am, for he grew up watching TV, *The Little Rascals*, *Leave It to Beaver*, reading *Spiderman* comic books, and going to matinee movies, while I did not. I grew up in my mother's pastoral version of America, decades old. When we are adults and our friends reminisce about their suburban childhoods, I am the one who has so little in common.

4

A small white house on Tucson's Westside, Barrio Hollywood, so named in the 50s because the junkies who hung out by the pay phone wore dark glasses *como el* James Dean. Three rooms in a line like a trailer: living room, bedroom, kitchen. Wood ceilings, painted-over linoleum floors, mismatched window frames salvaged from wherever. A row of salt cedars hedged the yard off from the street. It was 1972. I was eighteen, just back from Europe and feeling disoriented, no longer at home in my old life. I was sitting on an overturned five-gallon paint bucket. It was a warm day. I was watching Fernando and his cousin work on my car.

Can I fasten in my own mind the first time I met him? It wasn't this day at Johnny and Lupe's. No, of course not. It wasn't that day on the mall at the university. And it wasn't that party when we did the beer run in his old blue truck with the three back windows. No, none of those. Fernando says it was a day I don't remember, years before, maybe 1968, when I was fourteen. I was sitting on a curb with Walker, my high school boyfriend. I was stoned, so stoned, I don't remember Fernando, not even a glimpse. He says he stood there and talked to us for a long time, he says my hair was curly and shoulder length and I was a little chubby, wearing a pink dress. A little chubby? Is he sure? I seem to remember that I was thin, thin, always dressed in jeans and a black tee shirt, long hair. Bohemian. But maybe that was later.

Johnny and Lupe. What did I think when I met them? As I sat and watched? It felt like watching a movie. It felt like walking down a winding street in Montmartre, people gathered at the tables outside on the sidewalks, laughing, calling out to one another, kissing on the cheeks. The anthropologist does not discover, Anne Carson reminds us, she encounters. Travel is a quest for innocence, Pico Iyer says, we want to open ourselves to possibility. Does this explain my attraction?

The small white house, I remember. Fernando tells me he lived in a house just like this when he was a child. Here, in this neighborhood, he went to grade school. Here, at this church, he was baptized. Here, the bakery where they bought donuts and tortillas. Johnny was

Fernando's second cousin. I remember sitting on the paint bucket while they worked on my car, a '63 T-bird, baby blue. There were several children, small children, stair steps down, one after another, running barefoot out of the dark mouth of the doorway. I remember my bare feet in the powdery dirt, the ground speckled with sunlight, the children playing in Spanglish, their vowels rising like balloons in some poem.

Lupe was a witch (some said) or at least she had bewitched Johnny. Johnny was a brilliant mechanic. For a six-pack, he could fix anything. Lupe was beautiful in a Mexican calendar sort of way. Exotic. Full of fire. They fought all the time. There was electricity between them but nowhere to sleep.

Even then, Johnny was slightly crazy. You could tell he was half white. Hair like mine, light brown, frizzy when it rained. His eyes were green, a sign of mixed blood, they say. He'd been in a car accident when he was in high school and, until then, he had been headed for college on the GI Bill—his father, killed in World War II, he was his mother's hope. Then the head injury. Then Lupe. (No one knew which was worse.) Then too much drinking and too many children and not enough money and, by the time I met him, he was already hearing voices.

A few more years and he had the wild hair of John the Baptist. The cat in the alley was the devil. Airplanes flying overhead could tune into his thoughts and broadcast them on the radio. Lupe left him. He threw all of the furniture out of his mother's house and was washing it down with a hose when Fernando and his brothers arrived. They left the furniture in the yard to dry out and drove his mother to a relative's house, took Johnny out for a beer where they listened, for a long time, just listened, as he got Scripture all mixed up with his own sorrows.

How many days or months later, children found him dead in the schoolyard before the first bell rang. It was winter. He was cold. The cops said he had walked into the cross bars of the monkey gym and knocked himself out, but everyone knew they had beaten him. At the rosary, we could see the bruises on his face, barely covered by makeup. His children were there, they were older. Lupe was there, no one talked to her. The women kneeled inside and prayed the rosary. I went outside and stood in the dim circle of light on the porch while the old men told their stories.

I was a traveler, only half in the world, recording, remembering what I could see, relying on images. Perhaps this is why most of my memories are silent. I could understand only snatches of Spanish; English words brought everything into focus, but even English required interpretation. At home, for instance, I was never sure if people meant what they said, if their words matched whatever lay beneath them. Too many things left unspoken. Everything—gestures, facial expressions, sighs—required an act of translation. This feeling of disconnect was one I had come to prefer.

One of the old men in the circle was dressed *muy* sharp, creased pants, dress shirt, Ray Bans, a—¿*como se dice?*—an old-fashioned hat. A fedora. He had been in the Army and had seen the world. *Que suave*, he looked at me, laughing. *Que suave*, he said to Fernando, raising his eyebrows.

5

Fernando remembers the very first time he saw me. It was in a vision. He was twelve years old and lying on the couch in the house on Alameda. It was late afternoon and the light was tricky. In the square of the window, there was a girl, a white girl in a brown dress. At first, he thought she was the ghost of someone who used to live in the house, but then years later he saw me sitting on a curb with my boyfriend and he knew. I was the girl in the brown dress with French knots and a big white collar, her long honey-colored hair in braids.

In my dream, we are lying on our sides, flying through the night sky, flying through darkness. We are far above the world and I am a little frightened. Everything will be all right, he says. He puts the palm of his hand against my cheek. He whispers it again. Everything will be all right.

6

Fernando was sprawled across a beanbag chair. This was in a tract house on the Eastside, avocado shag carpeting, there may even have been lava lamps, Steve Miller on the stereo, the Allman Brothers. Eat a Peach. Fernando was drinking orange juice, no tequila for him, he was recovering from hepatitis. He'd heard I was in Europe. He'd heard I hadn't wanted to come back. (I hadn't.) He'd heard I was going to marry an Englishman. (That wasn't true.) He'd almost died. The whites of his eyes had turned yellow and so had his skin, his shit had turned white and his piss, black. He was six foot one and he weighed one hundred and twenty pounds. He could not open the door to the clinic without his sister's help. The doctor had said he should go to a hospital but his parents couldn't afford it.

He had almost died and I had been to Europe, where I hadn't missed dope at all, and so why start again? But we did. First just on Friday nights. Recreationally, we told ourselves. Instead of flowers or candy, he brought a dime paper when he came to my apartment. Even now, thirty years later, a kind of electricity, I remember. And then the floating. Anyone who's had Demerol for surgery understands the floating, what you would give for that, not to mention the Technicolor dreams.

But then, and who knows exactly when it happens, how it happens, when it's no longer something you want but something you need and so something you need to quit. What are the dividing lines? How did this happen to us, that's what you wonder. How could we have been so stupid? Time to quit, that's what you say. Over and over again you say this: when your arms get so sore; when you no longer get high, you only get well; when everyone is looking to rip you off; when you have no money; when you're getting evicted; when your car won't start or you run it out of oil (because who can afford oil?); when the cops come to your house in the middle of the night, the light on the helicopter so bright, it may as well be noon; when the junkie who's selling to you tells his kid to watch the TV but the kid hears the match and he turns his head and sees the flame beneath the spoon and there his mother is, standing up against the wall, checking the veins on her arms, and the dad stands up and walks over to the kid, all of five years old, and slaps him, hard, and says, I told you not to look. And you think, what the hell am I doing? Living in a bad movie?

Or maybe it's the day that Diane, just out of the hospital, her fourth miscarriage, overdoses, and you have to put her in the bathtub, run cold water over her to bring her out of it. And then you watch her get on the motorcycle behind her boyfriend and you know that could be your future. You could be Diane. Don't fool yourself. Don't think you're better than she is.

Or maybe it's something as simple as this: you're lying in bed and you have just enough for your morning wake-up and Fernando says, we have to quit. Something bad is going to come down. And this seems wise to you. Profound. And you look out the window of the motel room in the motel so rundown that they've filled the swimming pool with dirt and the ladders descend into dirt and you know he's right. Winter is the best time to quit.

7

The Hope Center, a storefront painted white. People in line for their morning medication, their nerves ragged, you could see that, the way they shifted from foot to foot, sniffled. Some of them were skinny, teeth missing; some were making deals, bumming smokes. Some were juggling toddlers. They looked old. Thirty, thirty-five, forty. *You mean this could be your life?* Inside, a high counter and a woman mixed the methadone in orange juice and then handed you a small white cup, watched as you swallowed the bitter medicine.

There we stood every morning for two weeks, even Sundays, across from the main library, in front of the convent. Who's the flower child, Buster Glass asked Fernando. He was on maintenance, we were in line for detox. I was smoking a cigarette. It was cold. I was wearing a thin black sweater I'd bought in London, a long India-print dress, I remember this, and macramé sandals.

No shit, Buster said, you some granola girl. Some flower child. It was true — although I never thought of myself that way — I worked in a boutique, painted my fingernails blue, made jewelry and took poetry classes. Buster Glass was an old black guy with white hair, worked construction with Fernando.

So you like bread more than tortillas, Carmen asked Fernando in Spanish. *¿Pan más que tortillas?* As if I couldn't understand her. As if she cared whether I could. This was, maybe, our first day in couples' group. Our second? Carmen wrapped in a pink yarn sweater. Her husband, Gato, just shook his head and whistled through his teeth. Cold, Carmen was cold. Then the waitress when we went to breakfast: *¿Que quiere ella? Ella* as if it was a dirty word. She looked through me. Every time.

All my life I'd thought people would prefer to be white, if they'd had a choice, but no, I was the outsider and it was personal. It had an edge, a tone. White people this, white people that. Stupid white people. I can't help it if I'm white, I said to Fernando, I'm not responsible for *all* the misery in the world.

They don't mean anything by it, he said. They must have forgotten you're white, he said, or they wouldn't say it in front of you. White people aren't the only ones who can be prejudiced, he finally said, oh so patiently, as if I were a child. I was a child. Like a child. But I couldn't hold it against them, my own ignorance and the ways of the world.

8

So, Homer said, today we're gonna talk about re-la-tion-ships. Homer was the fa-cil-i-ta-tor of the couples group. He talked like that, in separate syllables, and he didn't want any jive. No jive, Jones. No jonesing, Jones. This is detox, sucker, you're supposed to feel sick. He actually said jones, as in, how long you had your jones? I had mine ten years. You dig? Like it was a badge of honor. Word on the street, word to the wise: he was still using. No one trusted him. Everyone there, except for us, was on a court order so he could fuck with them. Now you tell me, Homer said, what makes you all stay together. He looked around the circle, at Carmen and Gato, at us, at the white guy who cried all the time and his girlfriend with the swimming-pool eyes. At Yaqui, the boxer, and his pregnant wife. Homer was waiting. You in a relationship? Or you just spoon partners? I want you to think about that. Who leads and who follows. Who's in control. Is it a matter of control? Homer pacing. Waiting. Everyone looking in their coffee cups. Gato cleaning his fingernails.

9

Tommy, the other counselor, his hands held in front of him, finger-tips pressed together, a black butterfly. What are you two doing here, he asked us, you don't belong here. You two can beat this. His face seemed ancient to me, as if in it I could find some truth about myself. I'd heard he was still using, too, but I didn't believe it. Not Tommy. He'd reached some other kind of calm. Didn't have any family, no kids, no wife, no girlfriend. So he'd quit for himself. This place, this is what he did, and then he rode the bus home to some small apart-ment where he lived by himself. I could imagine a whole life for him but, somehow, no matter how many times I imagined it, the end was always tragic. Something sad always caught up with him. Or maybe something sad had already caught up with him and, as kind as he was, had sucked everything out of him and now there was only paralysis, inertia, the inertia that was dope because, even when you weren't do-ing it, it was all you wanted. The inertia of absence, like the gap a lover leaves where nothing else matters.

10

Maybe the first time was in a schoolyard. Fernando and two of his brothers had organized a softball game and they'd brought all of his younger brothers and sisters to play. When was this? Before his family moved to the house on the Southside. Before Anna was born. I remember sitting under a tree with the youngest brother and sisters. How old were they? Under six, I think. The tree was leafy. I don't remember toy cars or dolls. What did we do? They were curious and asked me questions. I must have played little games with them. I must have sung songs, Itsy bitsy spider, Little bunny foo foo. I'd been a counselor at a summer camp. They liked me. Later, when Fernando and I were dating, after Anna was born, we would buy a sack of hamburgers on a Friday night and they would pile into the back of the old panel truck and we would take them to the drive-in. All six of them, sometimes a friend or two. Blankets and pillows and hamburgers and french fries. He'd back the truck into a good spot and then open the big back doors so they could watch the movie. *Sword in the Stone. Jason and the Argonauts.* Anna's face when she caught Fernando kissing me.

11

Fernando's face when he kissed me. Sometimes his hand trembled when he brushed my hair back from my forehead. Sometimes, when we were making love, his eyes studied mine right before he kissed me. He was memorizing me. When he left me off at my parents' house, he walked me to the doorstep, he kissed me on the forehead.

When he left me off at my parents' house after the two-week detox, he said: after we've both been clean for a month, we can see each other again. This was a rule he'd made up. Right then. On the spot. Do I have anything to say about this, I asked. No, he said. Otherwise, we'll just bring each other down.

I had pneumonia. We'd just come from the emergency room. I was in no shape to argue. I stood on the porch and watched until the blue truck got to the end of the street and turned. In my room, I lay on my bed. I had a fever. I tried to levitate the bottle of codeine out of my purse, the pills out of the bottle. I was so tired. I had come loose in time. I floated down the hall. Home again. Alone.

I 2

My mother said to me one thing she should not have said: *he doesn't love you*. It was a night in early spring, windy. Rain was coming. You could smell it in the dusty white blossoms of the pyracantha, in the desert creosote. The scents are always in the air, but only when rain comes is there enough moisture for us to smell them. It's another invisible thing about the world. Our failing: something present we cannot sense. The pyracantha was scratching at the screen of the window in my bedroom.

My mother said, he doesn't love you. Whither thou goest, I will go, she said. Thy people shall be my people. Are you ready for that? My father, his hands shaking, said, for God's sake, don't marry him. Every morning when I wake up, I will grieve for you.

I was outside and inside myself at once, as always happens in moments of extreme emotion. I was watching, disconnected, silent, trapped in my own limited understanding. I tried to imagine my father grieving every morning for the rest of his life. It seemed impossible.

The pyracantha was tapping at the window. My mother said, take only what you can carry. And then I saw that she was small and could not reach me. I hate it when you live in that part of town, she said, you may as well live in another country. What if you get sick or need me?

She was wondering how it had come to this. There, in my blue jeans and baggy sweater, scars on my arms, I must have been a mystery to her. Not the daughter she raised to go to law school, to graduate magna cum laude or, at the very least, to marry well. No, there I was, a stranger: a girl who made jewelry and took classes in poetry and Spanish and dated a Mexican, a girl who had been given everything, everything, and yet who seemed determined to throw all those advantages, all those gifts, away. Who is she, my mother must have wondered. What is so wrong with this life she's been given? Why is she angry? What does she want from me?

I wanted her to say things she could not say. I wanted the mother of my childhood to hold me, maybe it was as simple as that, as touch, but I was nineteen years old and this was an argument. I threw everything I owned into boxes. She said, once you cross the line, you never come back. Take only what you can carry. She had said that before, too, and she meant it. She could be strict. She had sealed off some part of herself long ago, long before I was born, I had always known that, I think. I had always known it was impossible for her to give me what I needed and, maybe, even then, I knew it was unfair for me to ask the impossible. One can give only what one can give. Nothing more. No matter how often you demand it. Or how much you need it. It isn't any different between mothers and children than between lovers or friends. Why should it be? My mother was a survivor. At all costs, she would keep her heart safe and sealed away, like a seed with a hard shiny husk.

But what I didn't know, then, was how to read beneath her words. I felt only her anger, not her pain. Or maybe I couldn't differentiate between the two. Maybe the room just felt airless and the pyracantha was tapping at the window and I wanted out.

13

It must have been a Sunday because, like a Sunday, like Christmas, the streets were mostly empty. You had to remember what you wanted on Saturday or you were out of luck. Simple as that. The streets were empty, the families inside their houses, gathered around tables. It was raining. When Fernando opened the door, I could see his mother and the children sitting on the mustard-colored couch. His youngest brother was kneeling in the middle of the living room, laughing. He had on a turquoise shirt and his hair was falling in his eyes. They looked at me for a minute but they were watching Lawrence Welk, maybe, or maybe Candid Camera. After all, it was a Sunday.

In his room, Fernando and I sat on the small single bed. He touched my hair. Oh, I've missed you, he said. The window was painted white to keep out the western sun. Two of his brothers moved their belongings out of the room, helped me carry my boxes in. There was a shelf and that's where I put my books, my bottle of lotion. My box of clothes, we shoved under the bed. His youngest sister Anna came in and said, is all of this yours? She held out one small finger and ran it along the spine of a clothbound book. She was three. Her dark hair fell across her forehead in a slant of thick bangs. *Is all of this yours?* Even when she is thirty-six, she will have the same doubt in her eyes. I will see it again and again in all the girls, in my daughter, in my nieces, in all the girl children who will follow, Anna's eyes. Doubt. Careful scrutiny. Even at three, she knew the world was not to be trusted.

If you're going to live here, Fernando said, we have to get married. My mother's Catholic. And then there are my sisters. And I said, Okay. But I was thinking, hmmm. Married. Hmmm. What if it doesn't work out? Well, if it doesn't work out, we would get divorced. That was how I thought back then. In steps. One two three. I didn't know anyone who was divorced but for someone so romantic as to run away, I could be practical.

He was the oldest of nine, remember, and so there were twelve of us in a small tract home on the Southside of Tucson, directly in the flight path of the airport and the Air National Guard. There was never any silence in that house. Too many children. Too much TV. The sixteen-wheelers on the freeway, background music. I always dreamed of planes when we lived in that house.

14

His mother said you should make a cross with the salt to bless the food. She cupped her hand over the bowl full of flour for tortillas. Like this. Just enough. Until you feel the grains between your fingers. Mornings spent in the yellow light of the kitchen, gathered at a table with his younger brother and sisters while his mother made breakfast and told stories about *la llorona*, about growing up in Tucson, how the river used to run, about his father and the Mexican Revolution. There were signs, she said. A dropped fork meant someone would visit. An egg with double yolks meant twins; one with blood meant someone would die. It was as if there were another world beneath this one, a world of spirits, things we couldn't always understand, things we could not see but that should be believed nevertheless. Voices we might listen to. Dreams and stories to guide us. And there was a way in which we should move through this world. Don't draw attention to yourself. Don't ask for more. Share. What does it matter if your house is clean, if your heart is black?

15

The neighborhood grocery. Del Monte's. Even the Lees spoke better Spanish than I did. Over the loudspeaker you couldn't tell at first if it was Chinese or Spanish. It just sounded choppy. The grocery store, a world of sounds that didn't mean anything, a different form of deafness or submersion in the self. Half the clues were missing. You had to watch people, their lips moving, the expressions on their faces. Happy? Sad? Gestures. Listen for key words. *Carne?* That way.

The soda bottles are lined up in cases under the front windows. Dusty. The aisles of canned goods, dusty. Don't forget cottage cheese. *Salsa Ranchera.* The produce is to the left but is wilted. The butcher is Betsy's mom. She's from Mexico. Her name is Emma. If she sees you, she will put a special price tag on the hamburger. When her husband gets angry and they argue, she protests, Oh, Louie, you know I don't understand English so good. He is such a big man, half French, half Sioux, that even when he's *not* in the driver's seat of their Mustang, it slants precariously to the left. His grandfather sat in the war party with Sitting Bull. There is a diary in French, but no one can read it.

This was in 1974. There were long lines at the gas stations. On the Southside of town, everyone was out of work. Windows got boarded up instead of replaced. Children without shoes hopped from shadow to shadow as they followed their mothers to the store. We went to the Food Bank and got bags of flour to make tortillas, dried milk for the children. We cut corn off the cobs and ground it in the *molinaro* to make tamales. We did laundry on the back porch in a wringer washer that had no wringer. Mint, *yerba buena*, grew under the faucet. The sheets were very long and hard to twist. The towels came out as gray as the soapy water. We hung the clothes on the line until they were dry and stiff and smelled of a dusty sun.

16

We are driving in his purple '65 Chevy through the dark streets of downtown, past the main library, ghostly white behind trees. Past the Hope Center, I watch it slide by, past the convent. You could go to school, I tell Fernando, if you wanted. I could help you.

Look, he says, I like my life. You want someone to go school, he says, you go. Look, he says, I don't need a white savior. (But maybe that was on another night.) Thanks anyways, he says.

This is all because of my parents, I know, my parents in the Italian restaurant on Fourth Avenue. They'd found the announcement of our marriage license in the newspaper and took us out to eat in celebration. Murals of Venice and Rome on the walls. Candles dripping thick wax down the sides of Chianti bottles. I'd ordered chicken cacciatore. My parents were trying. They said to Fernando, what are your plans for school? Surely you don't want to be in construction all your life.

Now we have left them behind on the sidewalk outside the restaurant, we have driven past the convent, past the *winitos* on the street corners and in the shadows of doorways. I crack the window and blow my smoke out in a stream, look at the houses, shacks, really, along South Tenth, plaster crumbling off the adobe, boards in the windows, tin roofs.

I can't believe he said that to me. *I don't need a white savior.* I can't believe he said it as if it were nothing.

Now we are driving past the Shamrock, a bar where he drinks on Fridays, where little kids come in, selling tamales and single red roses, and his friend, skinny Luis, dances with the big Indian women. He calls it pushing the *tanques* around. *Tanques*, do I get it? Yes, I say, but it's not funny. If you want to say they're fat, why don't you just say they're fat? You say other mean things.

Fernando tugs on my hair. (This is the way he apologizes?) I crack the window again and blow a deep sigh of smoke out toward the darkness. I do not put my hand on his thigh. (*That* is the way I answer.) Look, he says, we get married and you want everything to change.

Out the window, night slides by like time-lapse photography. Like when you're little and you squint your eyes at the Christmas lights and all you see is teary blurred color. I did want everything to change. I wanted to escape my parents' life, to enter another country, but I hadn't expected to find there barefoot children hopping from spot of shade to spot of shade as they followed their mother to the grocery.

17

Lim Bong's, the words bled through the whitewash on the walls outside. One of the grocers had been murdered with a cleaver. That half of the building, boarded up, was abandoned. Fernando's family, when he was a child, lived in the other half. At night, while they were lying in bed, the lights would suddenly go on in the old grocery store. They could hear the cleaver clacking on wood. Fernando told me these stories as we lay in bed at night, the tinny radio echoing through the vents from his sisters' room. We'd lie there in the dark, talking late into the night, all night, all of our stories, where each of us had come from, the ghosts we carried around inside. It is possible we didn't even get to know each other until after we were married.

Another year, they lived in the house on Alameda, the stucco fallen away, adobes exposed. With its tall arched windows, wooden floors, and fireplace, it was once a grand house. They hid their cousin from the cops, there, in the hollow pillars at the corners of the walls just as, long ago, someone must have hidden outlaws or treasure. The house on Alameda, that's where Fernando had first seen the spirit of me, standing in the light of the window.

When there was no money to pay the bills, they did their homework by candlelight; their mother leaned over into the fireplace and lifted the lid of the *olla* to check on the beans. She made tortillas outside under the *ramada*, the huge cast-iron *placa* smelled like burnt flour. When there was no money to buy clothing or shoes, they did not go to school.

Fernando, oldest of nine, walks next door with a bucket to get water from the neighbor's faucet. At dusk, he runs down the alley to the store for milk, and the *winitos*, who hide in the shadows of the yellow jasmine reach out and grab at him. In the morning, a *winito* or two, maybe the same ones, knock at the back door and his mother gives them cups of coffee, pieces of tortilla or bread. (You never know when one of them might be the Savior.) (Leave a light on in the window in case someone needs your help. *¿Quién sabe?* Who knows? You never know.) His father comes home late at night from the cantinas, tells them stories about *la llorona*, the coyote, the girl who danced with the devil. They all remember the hole in the wooden floor, the strange cat that appears one night and crouches on their father's chest, trying to suck the breath out of him while he sleeps. They all remember hunger.

18

The summer Fernando's mother saw *la llorona*, she was just a girl. They had sprayed down the dirt outside the house to cool the air, it was early evening. They had sprayed the dirt, packed it down with their bare feet until it was hard and polished as stone, they had taken the beds outside to sleep under the trees, behind the hedge in her grandparents' yard, and they all saw her, a woman dressed in white, floating down the street, like this, as if her feet weren't moving. That was the summer her two younger brothers died. First the older one and then the baby. The morning the baby was dying, her father was sitting at the table in the kitchen. He felt so helpless. And then the older one came back on a breeze through the open window and told him he would take care of the baby.

In the morning, in the kitchen, in the yellow light. I sit at the table and watch Dora gingerly heat the tortillas on the gas stove. She pours a spot of coffee into a cup of warm milk and gives it to Anna with her tortilla. I stir in the sugar. Anna peers at me over the edge of her cup. Sometimes I think Dora tells me these stories simply because I am a willing listener. I love the way whole histories open up before my eyes, one or two details and I can imagine a life. Sometimes, I think she is initiating me into the family, showing me a history other than the one I've been taught, saying to me, listen, I know what you think, that the world has a smooth seamless surface but, really, everything goes much deeper than that. There is a tangled web that roots us, makes us who we are, limits or lifts us. What happens to us isn't a matter of simple will. There are powers beyond our control and sometimes all we can do is give in. Have faith. *Ojalá. Que será, será.*

When her mother, Grace, was a young girl, her own mother died, and there were younger sisters to care for. In the mornings, Grace would go outside to get the water and when she came back in, her younger sisters, their hair, it would already be brushed and braided. Who braided your hair, she would ask them, and they said it was their mother. Grace was old enough to understand that their mother was dead, what that meant, and so one morning, she went out for only a little while and when she came back in, her mother was there.

Standing there. She had just finished braiding the youngest girl's hair and she reached out to Grace, but Grace was afraid and she flinched and so when her mother touched her temple, it burned, her fingers were so cold, they burned. And after that, and for all the rest of her life, Grace got headaches, there, on her temple, where her mother had touched her in anger. After that, her mother never came again and the priest put a glass of holy water on the mantle. He told Grace, when the water evaporates, her soul will be in Heaven. It takes a long time to evaporate when a mother dies, a long time, because she does not want to leave her children.

19

Fernando's Tía Norma lives in a low house next to a dry river in *Barrio Sabaco*. Only Mexicans, Fernando tells me, give neighborhoods names like that. *Barrio Sabaco*. Neighborhood of the Armpit. They are allowed to keep pigs and goats in their yards, chickens and ducks, and so the air smells musty, fertile, stinky like an armpit. His Tía Norma married Poncho when she was fifteen years old. In the picture, he is in uniform, his hat in his hand, older than she is, and she is a girl, really, just a girl, standing between him and her sisters, smiling. Norma is Dora's younger sister and she is tall like their mother Grace was tall and she has their mother's white white skin and black hair just as our son, when he is grown, will have white skin and straight black hair.

The house, set beneath a grove of old mesquite trees, is long and rambling, full of children, a room built on as each is born, perhaps. There is a big enamel pot of *menudo* on the stove. It is New Years. The steam rises in Norma's face as she stirs it. Her hair, I remember, is drawn back into a bun. Her eyes crinkle at the corners. *Menudo*, squeeze in lemon and the clear broth turns cloudy, sprinkle in green onion and cilantro. *Pan birrote*, little crusty breads, legacy of Napoleon's Mexico.

One step down into the dining room with the long wooden table. Fernando's *tata*, Rodrigo, deals the cards for a game of twenty-one. Rodrigo is a little man in his eighties with long white hair and a white goatee. Fernando tells him that I've been to Paris. He remembers Paris. He rakes his fingers through his goatee and cackles. He remembers enough French to ask me if I'd like to take a walk in the moonlight. *Au claire de lune. Une promenade.* He is pleased that he remembers the words.

He'd been there in World War I. They had come down to the ranches, looking for sharpshooters, and he'd been chosen, but then they made him work in the mess, cooking for the other soldiers, because, *tu sabes, era mexicano*. After the war, when they arrived in Paris, the French crowded along the wide boulevards, cheering. Oh, those French women, he said, how they loved American soldiers! Then, in Spanish: the children, they had no shoes, nothing to eat, and the soldiers gave them food, bought them shoes, and there were red flowers in the window boxes and the women plucked the flowers and they leaned out of the windows and threw them, the flowers floating down onto the soldiers in the streets.

Rodrigo had a woman in Paris, and a son, and then he came home and married Fernando's grandmother and for years Grace sent letters and money to the woman in France, to the first son of her husband, a child she would never meet. Even when her own baby sons died, even when they lived in a tent during the Depression and had to spray the dirt floors with water and pack the dirt down with their feet until the earth was smooth and hard like polished clay, even when there was barely enough to feed her own children, she sent money to a woman and a child in France.

They say Rodrigo had known since he was a child that he would marry Grace. He had seen her when she was a baby. He was twelve years old, lived with his parents, ranch hands on the *Rancho del Oso*; at the neighboring ranch, he had leaned over her, an infant in a crib, daughter of the schoolteacher at Picacho, and declared he would marry her. Of course, he couldn't have known she would die before him, that lying on his deathbed in the V.A. hospital, his children and grandchildren standing around him, he would be waiting for her, waiting for Grace, he said, to come along and pull him out of this life by his socks.

Norma was ill for a long time, too, diabetes, an amputation. Their children had moved into their own homes by then and Norma had filled her house and back porch with birds, colorful birds, and then, like her mother, Norma died before her husband. Poncho was left with the music of birds and grandchildren. A *nieta*, just toddling, who brought him messages from Norma, a crumpled photograph, a look in her eyes, a gesture.

20

Before Dora dies, and she will not die until she is in her eighties, she will spend her time visiting with the dead. They will be more real to her than the living. I can see them, she'll say, they're sitting in my nana's garden, behind the high hedge, but I don't remember, *mi'jo*, have they passed on? Or are they still with us? Dora's stories will become mere fragments of memory, a train whistling at night, rumors of Pancho Villa visiting neighbors, a lost gold nugget as large as a man's fist. The grandmother from Italy, Petra? Pietra? Another grandmother—or great-grandmother?—who came as a small child from California by horseback, they were driven from their Spanish land grants by white settlers hungry for land and gold. They had to drive their cattle down into Mexico and then back up through Nogales. They lost nearly everything. *Los Ronquillos.* Dora's grandmother had ridden horses since she was a girl, she had a way with horses, used to sleep with them in the barn, sometimes, and there are other details about her life, other stories Dora used to tell, but now they are lost and Dora's grandmother is simply a girl who rode a horse all the way from California and settled, with her family, in the Rincons, the mountains east of Tucson, until those ranches, too, were taken away by white Americans with their false deeds. How I hated them then, Dora will say when she's very old, my grandmother showed me the papers and I saw how they had taken everything as if it were theirs to take! Ppfffp! She'll blow air through her lips, swat as if swishing a fly away. That is as much time as bitterness is worth, she seems to be saying, as much time as that. Loss does not have to leave us unmoored. Better to remember than to forget. To remember sitting next to her nana's chair in the garden, behind the high hedge. To remember her nana's hair, so long, so heavy, down to the middle of her back, but she wore it up, and like mine, Dora will marvel, it was dark. No gray in it! I look in the mirror and I think, *who's that? What happened? Why did I have to marry a younger man? Tell me that.* She motions to the walker she refuses to use. *He thinks he can tell me what to do.* She looks off to the side, as if there is someone in her peripheral vision, someone who might have an answer.

2 1

After she dies, Fernando's father will dream that he sees her off in the distance. He will wave to her, but she won't respond. In the dream she is far away, on a hill or standing behind a gate with a number of other people, one is a small boy. It is a tall gate, perhaps made of black wrought iron, and Maurilio is worried that there is an argument and so he walks over there. Dora doesn't notice him. Her back is to him and she is still talking to the other adults. He asks the boy, is there a problem? Oh, no, the boy says, no problem. You just don't belong here.

Anna will dream that her mother and Tía Amelia are talking. They are sitting in chairs under a tree; they are whispering about Norma. She's just got her wings, they say. Just then Norma appears and she is very pleased with herself. Turn around, they say — so Anna can see — and she does and there they are, two small white wings. Just nubs, really. Why are they so small? Anna asks and Dora gives her that look, the one where she peers right over the edge of her glasses: they've just come in, well. They have to grow.

Fernando will not dream of his mother, not for months after she dies. Why is this, we'll wonder. He thinks she might be busy visiting other people, people who need her more than he does. Right before she died, she heard a baby crying. Then she opened her eyes and said, I felt something pass through me. And then she closed her eyes and then she stopped breathing.

22

The first time Dora saw Maurilio, he was standing in the yard, his shirt off, he was pouring water from a clay pot over his head and his hair shone copper like a penny in the sun. She thought, *who is that stranger?* and immediately felt a chill of recognition. She was twenty-four, worked as a riveter on the airplanes, and had seen her future. It was not what she had expected. He was not supposed to be in the picture. No, there is corn in the picture. She is standing alone in her trousers and white blouse. The corn is taller than she is. She has always been independent, has never wanted a boyfriend, has been driving since she was fourteen, has been all the way to Yuma, has worked in the houses of rich people, taking care of their babies since she was twelve. She has always been able to see in glimpses and in dreams what will happen, but when she was small, her mother had slapped her for seeing her aunt's death, so she learned to say nothing. Still, she knows silence can't stop what will come: when she sees the man with copper hair, she knows the picture has changed.

23

Maurilio Miguel grew up in Michoacan, on a large hacienda built around a central courtyard. Open the huge wooden doors and there it is, an oasis. In the courtyard there are huge trees and from them hang clay pots of water to cool in the breeze; there are birds, a cacophony of songs, flowers so large and vibrant they have tongues. There is a church on the ranch, long and low and white, built in the shape of a cross. Above the altar, Christ carries the cross, stumbling, one knee on the ground. When Maurilio was five, the *Federales* came out to the ranch and he hid in the cellar of the chapel with the statues. The statues were white and cold, the cellar was dark, and he could hear the hollow sound their boots made on the wooden floor above his head, the fine dirt sifting down with the light.

Dora tells me I remind him of his mother because of my light-colored hair and the way I braid it, because my maiden name was Coryell and hers, Curiel. His mother, like me, was afraid of thunder—Dora always tells us this story when the monsoons come and it's raining and she and the children and I are in the living room, waiting for the thunder to stop. Maurilio, when he was a child in the hacienda, Dora tells us, used to hide with his mother and little sister; they would crawl under the dark table in the *sala* and hide until the storm had passed.

Maurilio's father, Carlos, had been a *Cristiano*, one who defended the church. In the early 1920s, when the government was looting and burning the churches, Carlos had gone with other men to defend a nearby town. After the *Federales* left, while smoke was still rising from the rubble, he rode up and saw a beautiful woman standing in the ruins. As if in a movie, he helped her onto the back of his horse and they galloped away and fell in love. She was the daughter of a wealthy German merchant and he was the son of a Spanish *hacendado*. They fled to California and married, had two children before returning to Mexico. Late one night, Carlos was in town, working in the family's trucking firm, locking up the office, and someone shot him in the back. Maurilio, four or five at the time, remembers his German grandfather at the wide wooden doors of the hacienda. He has come to collect his daughter and granddaughter. Maurilio he leaves behind.

Later, when Maurilio is thirteen, he will get into a gunfight with a *Federale*, perhaps the same one who killed his father, and his uncles will dress him as a woman, smuggle him out of Michoacan to Mexico City, where he will live for a year with ancient aunts in a large house with servants. There are high walls he is never allowed to see over. Bowls of water on the table, you squeeze lemon in and then rinse your fingers. There is *mole, camarones* float in a red sauce, mangos and papayas are sweet. The old women wear black and rustle like angry nuns from room to room.

It is a relief to leave even though he has to be dressed, again, as a woman, and smuggled across the border, even though he is left alone at fourteen in California, where he will learn English and find work mounding dirt over stalks of asparagus so they will stay white and tender. Where he will drive trucks, taking food to relocation camps for the Japanese, where he will fall in love and have a son and leave them both. Where he will wear a Zoot suit and fight with the sailors and end up in jail for stabbing a policeman. Where, at the age of twenty-four, he will reinvent himself: move to Arizona and work on the roofs mopping hot tar, one hundred and twenty-five degrees in the summer, easy; he will learn to read and write English; he will marry, raise nine children. He will never look back. The past, like Mexico, is a place to be *from*: he is *mexicano, pero de los estados unidos*. His name is Mike.

24

Sometimes Fernando's father will tell his own stories and then his mother will roll her eyes as if to say, don't believe a thing. *¿Quién sabe?* It could all be lies. We'll be sitting in the kitchen, the talk winding its way around. You never ask a direct question, I've learned, because then no one wants to answer. They want to tell their own stories in their own time for their own reasons. And so Dora is telling us about being a riveter on the planes and that her boss called her Frenchie and then Fernando says something about his dad taking food out to the relocation camps and this is when his father's mind takes a turn toward Mexico. When he was thirteen, he says, he carried a gun. He had a horse shot right out from under him. He was taking seed from one part of the ranch to another and they ambushed him, killed his horse, one bullet went through his calf, and he just lay there, pinned by the horse, until his uncle found him the next morning. The *laguna* in Guanajuato, he says, was as wide as from here to Picacho and as long as from here to Nogales. In the rainy season, in January, they would close the floodgates and the land would be covered with water. They never had to irrigate. They grew everything. Wheat as tall as a man. He holds his hand up, six feet, to show us. He is leaning with his back against the sink and his hands are dark, stained from working on the roofs, the fingers curved, tar under the nails no matter how much he scrubs them. We had two ranches, he says, but we lost the one in Guanajuato because my grandfather held the deed by himself. There, in Guanajuato, we had grown corn, beans, everything, and we had five hundred head of cattle. But we were forced to give up that ranch, we had to move to the one in Michoacan where there was no lake. There, if there was a good rainy season, the land would produce, but it was more arid and there had been drought after drought, banks closed every day, this was during the Depression, every day we lost twenty-five head of cattle. There was no work. The *campesinos* had nowhere to go. Whole families wandered from ranch to ranch, looking for work, for a place to stay, stealing to feed themselves. Ranchers said anyone caught on their land was rustling. You could ride across central Mexico and see men hanging from trees.

25

I am *la guera*, which sounds like la wetta, which is slang for *la rubia*, the blonde one, polite for *la gringa*, but means, literally, the fair one. That's what Fernando tells me it means, the fair one. When we are at his Tía Norma's house and the screen door slaps shut behind the boys, his younger cousins, who are chasing each other out into the yard, and I hear them say *la guera*, I know they mean me. He has a cousin who is also called Guera, because her skin is so white, but I have the *la* before my *guera*, which I know has its own significance, like *la reina*, the queen, as in she thinks she's *the* queen, the only one, and so at the same time it's as if I'm singled out or think I ought to be, a kind of joke, maybe, but this is a new mask, a new way of being invisible while being in plain sight. I am simply who I appear to be, marked only by my appearance. I have become that surface. When I'm riding on the old round green bus down South Sixth Avenue, the bus with the windows pulled open, no air conditioning, the bus so crowded that there is standing room only and we may as well be in Italy or Mexico, and we pass the *carniceria* and the *tortilleria* and the storefronts painted bright yellow or orange or pink with blue letters and black wrought-iron bars over the windows, and the music of Spanish is all around me, I am *la guera*. When I hold in my hands at work the African trade beads, the shells, the turquoise beads, when I iron the clothes and dust all the vases and sculptures and bowls, when I sweep the front walk and move the dust mop under the display cases and write up the sales tickets and give the rich old ladies their change or try on the embroidered dresses so they can see how their granddaughters might look in them, I am *la guera*. Something is changing and, even though, soon, someday, I will become Beth again, I will never be exactly the same Beth. It has something to do with this sojourn, with this moving through my day in a completely different rhythm, surrounded by new sounds and colors and air, as if I have chosen to become someone else in another life in another country and, in choosing an exterior path, have set interior change in motion. When I lie on the bed after work and put my feet up on the wall because my ankles are swollen, when I lie in the sun, my hand across my belly, I know I will never be the same person again and it has everything to do with being *la guera* and everything to do with the fact that underneath my hand there is a swimmer, a not-child, his eyes blinking at the shadows of my fingers.

26

We have the same dream on the same night. It is around this time, I'm sure, because we are still living in the bedroom in Fernando's mother's house, the room with the windows painted white. In the dream, we are walking through a field of alfalfa, out in the middle of nowhere, but surrounded by a white picket fence. Off in the distance, we see rugged mountains and a dark wall of a forest. There is a rasping noise, as if a large prehistoric insect were flying over, but when we look up we see a biplane with canvas wings, the pilot is a woman, her long yellow scarf trailing through the air like a silken ribbon. She is waving to us, waving as she flies over, and the tiny man sitting behind her is waving, too. He has a funny leather football helmet on his head. Suddenly red comets come shooting out of the summer sky; they look like flames or firecrackers and are quite beautiful. The comets wake me; I wake Fernando. He opens his eyes. He says, you missed it—there was this round metal thing, like a satellite, it floated down out of a cloud and landed next to us in the field. Then it started humming and a little ticker tape was coming out of it. It was in some other language. I could barely understand it. It said, you will have two children and their names will each have seven letters. But, he says, you woke me up before I could read them.

27

A knock on the window at night means Fernando's brother needs money. Marty, he has black marks snaking down his arms, the last one to try heroin, the first to get hooked. When we quit, he couldn't, no matter how hard he tried. Marty, the girls love him, he has eyes like Elvis, but they turn green when he's high. His voice gets husky. He'll steal the battery out of your car if he needs to, the rings off his mother's fingers. Marty, all *sentido, tú sabes*, one of those men who can tell a sad story.

Men pounding on the front door at night means Marty owes someone. Fernando sits up, swings his long legs over the side of the bed and pulls his jeans and cowboy boots on. Every night, before we go to sleep, he takes his belt with the heavy brass buckles out of the belt loops and leaves it lying on the floor by the bed, ready, a weapon. You can snap a knife out of a man's hand. He can't reach you.

But what about a gun?

I am always afraid Marty will do something and Fernando will get killed; Marty will do something and the family will suffer the consequences. It's the way things work in life, if not in stories, the ironic universe at our door.

Men pounding on the front door. The small lamp casts a triangle of light in the corner of the room. The girls are crying down the hall. We hear the angry voices. It is midnight, the blue quilt tented over my legs as Fernando leaves to help his father answer the door. There is no phone in the house. Imagine. No phone. No way of reaching police we would never call even if we had one.

28

The courtroom is in South Tucson, the benches are smooth wood, pews, just like in church, and when the judge enters, we stand. He seems kind and so I have hope for Fernando, who has just found out there is a warrant out for his arrest. Traffic tickets. Unpaid traffic tickets, but he's never been stopped, and so he'd asked Marty, did you use my name? But Marty had said, why would I use your name when I can make one up just as easily? Don't you think I have an imagination?

When we come out of the courthouse, the sun has made the world a flat yellow. The car is hot — hot upholstery, sizzling chrome. I drape my arm over Fernando's shoulders and blow softly in his ear. He scrunches his shoulder up and gives me a grin. But how can we go back to his mother's at midday and go into the bedroom? Besides, he has to go and get a letter from his boss to prove he was at work when all those moving violations took place. So he knows I'm teasing. And I know he doesn't want to talk about Marty. He didn't mention Marty to the judge, not his name, not that the car belonged to Marty's girlfriend, not even the fact that he has a brother. He must figure Marty couldn't risk a traffic ticket but what I want to ask is: doesn't this feel like betrayal?

Fernando doesn't remember a time before Marty was born. No memory before Marty's birth when he was two. No playing between the hollyhocks, no mint under the water faucet, no nana, no mom, no puppies, no fresh tortillas, no oompah oompah of Mexican music from down the street. No self. *Nada.* Nothing before Marty.

In the old days Fernando's whole family lived in the same neighborhood on the west side, his nana, his tata, all his aunts and uncles and cousins. Small houses with porches, just like the ones we are driving past, they would sit for hours in the evenings, talking. When he was young, he would lie in bed and listen, Spanish slipping over him, soft and comforting as a breeze. Everyone was poor, everyone grew food in their gardens, raised chickens, cooked huge *ollas* of beans outside on their fireplaces. He remembered going into his nana's house after school, how there'd be a stack of fresh tortillas on the counter. The smell of flour, warm, slightly burnt on the *placa*. Once, he'd gone over early in the morning and surprised her at her dressing table. She was sitting with her back to him and her hair was long, down to the ground. He'd never seen it down. He wasn't sure it was her. *Nana?* he'd called and she turned, suddenly, *Boo!* out from under that curtain of hair.

Once, when he was about six, they'd all been sitting at the breakfast table bugging his mom for food and there wasn't any and suddenly, as she was standing there, her face went slack and she began to fall, heavily, in slow motion, falling and falling, her eyes open but not seeing. He'd thought she was dead. They were staying at his nana's house, he doesn't remember why, and so when his nana came into the kitchen to see what had happened, he went into the living room with his brothers and sister. Who was the youngest? He doesn't remember. Maybe Terri. Maybe Terri was the baby, so there were four of them then, and they all stayed in the living room, playing as if it hadn't happened. He kept looking at the door, afraid to go into the kitchen to see her. When the ambulance men came, they carried her out on a stretcher, his nana trying to straighten her nightgown, his mom's arm hanging, her face, she still wasn't there.

A nervous breakdown is what his nana told him and Fernando worries it will happen again. It will happen because of Marty. But his mom just says that Marty needs her more than the others. There's always one who needs you more, she says, and somehow you end up giving the most to him. She doesn't know why this is, but she has her theories. Maybe if she hadn't broken her leg when she was pregnant with him, maybe if the next child hadn't come along right away. She searches, always, for reasons. Had she done something or failed to do something? I want to tell her what anyone would say, that she shouldn't make excuses for him. That she should expect more. But I'm learning to be quiet about Marty. What do I know? He acts like a bull on the outside, she says, but that's not what I'm worried about.

That Marty, I say. I can't believe you're going to let him get away with it. I wish I had a cigarette, something to play with as we drive, but I've quit smoking. I fiddle with the car radio. I put my hand on Fernando's thigh. I wonder what it would have been like to live in this neighborhood, then, when the families went back generations, when everyone knew everyone, when everyone took care of everyone, when it was so clear if someone was an outsider.

29

Light dances in Anna's dark hair. Children are running in the street and airplanes buzz overhead, big black ants scurry in a line on the sidewalk. A man washes his red car, the suds dripping down. The air is alive with the neighborhood children's high thin voices. Anna reaches into the dark mouth of the mailbox and pulls out the mail. Nope, her *Sesame Street* magazine hasn't come yet. Maybe tomorrow, I tell her, and we march, one two one two one two, our feet getting powdery with dust, back into the house.

There is a baby towel in a patch of sunlight on the kitchen table, and next to the towel, the baby powder and clean clothes. Fernando's sisters are bathing Marty's baby in a large mixing bowl. Teresa holds the baby's head in the palm of one hand while Sylvia shampoos her hair. Patti is cooing, calming the baby, looking into her eyes and smoothing the water and suds over her arms and tummy. Anna holds my lotion in her hands. It smells like lemons, she says, her brown eyes round. Right here, she says, pointing to the label, it says, not for babies, for big girls, like Beth and Anna. When I was old, she says, and you were little, I let you use my lotion.

Those days in the yellow rooms of his mother's house, a world of stories and spirits, a world you could not control. What would come, would come. *Que será, será.* Don't draw attention to yourself. Be careful what you say, it might come back on you. Be careful what you wish for. Be careful. Be careful if you're pregnant and you're mad at someone, the baby might turn out like him.

I am in the bathroom, brushing my hair, braiding it. When I was old and you were little, Anna says, I had sunshine hair like yours. But then it got burnt. I look down at her, so used now to being with people with dark hair and dark eyes. Anna, I tell her, I would much rather have your hair, your pretty hair, and I lift her up so she can see herself in the mirror. See how it's so pretty and we haven't even brushed it yet. But seeing her face next to mine, I am surprised by my own pale reflection, by my blue eyes, and I realize I had expected some sort of transformation, not to be darker, not exactly, but not to be so white, either.

30

Que será, será seems to me, even then, even though I can't articulate it, a necessary fiction, a way to comfort ourselves, but it also, sometimes, makes me feel as if I'm in a small airless room. Fate, I resist the idea. To be fated means to have no choice. And so faith, does faith mean giving into fate? Accepting that things could *not* have been otherwise? This is what I don't understand. *Que será, será.* I'm not sure I believe it. Not sure I want to believe it. And yet it seems a great comfort, these stories. Believing them. Telling them. Even the ritual of telling them. Dora's face at the kitchen table, I want that kind of calm, am drawn to it, love listening. The words wash over me, into me, lulling me — until I come up against something I cannot accept, like Marty's inability to change. Unable, I think, only because he does not want to. *What will be, will be* seems, then, an excuse, a lie, something we believe and in our believing make so, but only because admitting the alternative is too painful.

31

Imagine the house, a large California bungalow, built around the turn of the nineteenth century, two stories, a wide green roof, attic windows, and a deep front porch with stone pillars. The Shelter Care is a temporary stop for lost children, thrown-away children. This is where we live and work after Michael is born. When we stand in front of it that first day, I am twenty-two, Michael, eighteen months, slung on my hip. It is an old house in an old neighborhood, once genteel, but now full of bars and head shops, hippies and the homeless, street people, we call them. The smell of patchouli and marijuana smoke waft through the air. We are qualified to be houseparents because we are ex-junkies, something that, even at the time, seems laughable. Oh, we've also been through the training at Juvenile Court, so we are certified, someone has certified us, although in my heart, I don't feel certified. The first time a kid calls me Ma'am, I look to the right of me as if I expect to see a grown-up standing there.

Dina, our first, her father white, her mother Mexican. What was the story? Too much alcohol. Maybe drugs. Maybe jail. The old litany. Then Veronica, tiny and dark-skinned, black eyes, her mother deported back to El Salvador. She lived with an old couple she called Nana and Tata in a small house in the roughest part of town. Domestic violence, but she was the one accused. Kenny, a handsome kid with dark curly hair and a big grin. Trish, blonde bangs falling in her eyes, won't bathe. She has been on the road for weeks, hitching rides with truckers. Body odor has become her first line of defense. Paul, the redhead, who had to cut his father down when he found him hanging in the basement. Paul, on suicide watch. Kenny, too, here for protection. His life has been threatened.

When the children come, they are sullen, they are angry. They sit on the couch. Middle of the night, middle of the day, doesn't matter. They are like cats, still inside, watching, eyes tracking everything that moves, muscles tensed, tails twitching. It's a matter of survival. It's dangerous to get attached, to open up, to confide. Everyone must first be measured. Everyone is found lacking.

Michael, who isn't a baby any longer but is not yet two, is still the center of his own world. He has fat moon cheeks and dark eyes and soft feathery hair. He runs around with his hands tucked into the bib of his Oshkosh B'gosh overalls. He hoots. He knows exactly thirty-two words. He is never afraid. He will throw the ball to anyone. Stop right in front of them, lean back from the waist, the way that toddlers do, big plastic ball between his outstretched arms, and shout before shoving it through the air. He is the only one they trust.

32

Wake up the kids. Make breakfast. Throw the windows and doors open, put on the radio, Peter Frampton, Aerosmith, Lynyrd Skynyrd. Help the kids with chores. Sweep, mop, wipe down counters. Bathrooms. No one wants to clean bathrooms. Watch the baby, oh the girls all love to watch baby Michael and he loves the girls. Wash the clothes in the washer out back. Hang everything on the line. Watch it so the transients don't steal anything, they are that quick. Morning group. Try not to be the ambulance rescuing everyone. Woo-ooo, woo-ooo, woo-ooo, the counselor says, here comes the ambulance. Make lunch. Go to the Y. Swim. Play basketball. Put Michael down for a nap. Afternoon group. Do the grocery shopping. Make dinner. Play pool on the donated pool table. Watch TV? Okay, for one hour. When the hot-water heater goes out, heat big pans of water on the stove for dishes and baths. When it's cold, make a fire in the fireplace and roast marshmallows. Tell ghost stories. Set traps for the mice. Bed checks. Answer the door at midnight. Do intake.

33

On the night Veronica runs, the house is blazing with lights from every window. Anyone passing by would see, so clearly, there has been, *is*, an emergency. Fernando, Kenny, Paul, and Trish set out on foot, up and down the streets, over to the park where the street people hang out, up and down the dark side streets and alleys. Dina and I can hear them. We are sitting on the back porch with Michael, our toes in the dust, we are waiting in case Veronica comes home. Then we decide to walk along Fourth Ave., past the bars and closed shops, down to the Dairy Queen where, Dina tells me now, sobbing, a half an hour too late, Veronica was supposed to meet *el negro*. An older guy, her boyfriend. *El Negro*. Maybe a pimp. Or maybe it's a nickname. She met him at the Spanish Well, a bar down on South Sixth where the hookers hang out.

Dina carries Michael in her arms. We are both barefoot, wearing, probably, shorts and tank tops, our long hair hanging down our backs. Dina's mascara smeared below her eyes. Maybe we both look like drug addicts, like runaways. I feel something close to love, a tenderness for her; it's as if we merge, but how can I tell you who she is? She has to be a character for you to remember her. What quirky things does she say? Does she tilt her head before speaking? Are her eyes a special shade of brown? Is her patience with Michael endearing? Does her weakness for getting high engender sympathy? But maybe she has been too marked by abandonment to be anything but timid. She will disappear and allow me to project onto her, blank canvas that she is at fifteen, any characteristics I want.

34

Sammy loves the cockatiel. It flew in the open window, landed on his shoulder, its white wings opening and settling, opening and settling. Sammy plays pool with the bird perched next to his ear where his dark hair curls. He's fourteen and likes women, likes to pinch a pretty girl on the butt, likes to show us how he can disco. He pulls a creased photo from his wallet, there he is, a skinny Puerto Rican kid standing with his arm around a plump white woman. She sure be ugly, Paul says. What you be, a red-haired nigger? Sammy says, kiss my ass. Every time.

Trish puts on eye shadow. Leaning forward over the sink, trying not to squint as the cigarette smoke floats up between her and her image in the mirror, she smoothes the powder over her eyelid with her fore-finger. Eye shadow, bright blue, sometimes teal, then, midnight blue mascara. Mascara in Spanish means mask, I tell her, *más cara*, more face. Just because you don't wear any, she says.

Later, she leans back against the pool table, a seductress from an old afternoon movie. How would I make this shot, she asks Kenny, tilting her head so her bangs fall away from her eyes. Kenny, our little dope pusher, says, bat those baby blues. Is this how you hold the stick, she asks. I can show her how to hold the stick, Sammy says, elbowing Paul. His left eye wanders. His cockatiel has flown away. He is lonely.

The pool table takes up all the space in the room with the fireplace. Perhaps it used to be the parlor, perhaps the baby grand stood next to the front window so you could look at the mountains and trees, at people passing on the sidewalk, while you played. Now you have to be careful when you make a side shot that the back of the cue doesn't go through the side window, the window that looks out on the desert elm and the apartment next door. At night, shadowy figures go in and out of that apartment. One night a man with one leg, his other cut off at the hip, was running from the street to the apartment, leaping on the one leg, it stretched out and he landed, it stretched out again, he landed, like an image from a dream or a movie. Kenny saw him, too, this look on his face like wonder. Kenny, here for protection because one night during a drug deal gone bad, he saw them throw a blanket over this guy's head and then shoot him.

35

Sammy was kicked out of the last group home for molesting a younger child. (Is this something I didn't consider? Putting my own child in danger?) The counselor leans back in his chair and clucks his tongue against his partial plate. That's DES for you. Just dropped him off. Tires smoking! He makes a cuckoo sign with his finger and grins. Sammy's a quart low, he says. A quart low. Two quarts low. Running on empty. Screws loose. That's how we talk here. The other counselor says humor is a form of self-defense. You don't want to get attached.

I don't let myself get attached. In moments of crisis, I never break down. At times when others might be emotional, I swallow. I tamp things down. I choose not to feel but to observe. I have this ability, I realize, to give myself over to fantasy, to love the fictions, the details of the kids' lives, to have intense relationships with them for days or weeks and then to let go completely. Oh, there might be a few moments where a hole opens in my heart, a few days where I feel them hovering just over my right shoulder, almost as if they're dead, but I tell myself that soon, I won't even miss them. I won't even be able to imagine their faces. I tell myself they will fade and fade and fade.

Two walls of the office are glass, the fan swirls the smoke from the counselors' cigarettes, shafts of morning light slice through the tamaracks, through the smoke in the air. This is the first I've heard of molestation and Sammy has been with us for three days, a long weekend. The screen door slaps shut as the kids take out the garbage, hang throw rugs on the line. I get up and go into the kitchen. Fernando is in the pantry. I tell him about Sammy. Good thing we do bed checks, he says. Goes with the territory, he says. Michael, chair pulled up to the sink, is helping two of the girls wash dishes. Just where I've left him, but I take him back out to the meeting with me. A red toy truck. Michael plays with a red toy truck at my feet.

36

A child, the counselor says, *is* her feelings. The most essential, most authentic self to a child is the way she feels and so if she's told to deny her feelings, if she's told they don't matter, to be quiet, then she gets the message that *she* doesn't matter. She disappears. Or there's a disconnect between mind and body and, if there's a disconnect, if the body is not the self, then what does it matter? You can do anything to the body, then. You can stick needles in it. You can prostitute it. You can deprive it of food, burn it with your cigarette, give your stepfather sexual access. You can drown it in alcohol.

I don't want to get attached, but I want to watch, which makes me, what? A voyeur? Someone consumed with other people's sadness? But maybe it's because when I was their age, I wasn't conscious. I was anesthetized. I couldn't watch myself, connect with myself—I remember looking at my own arm once and thinking, this is my arm? I am inside this body?—and so now, maybe, I think that in watching them I will learn something about myself. And there is a way in which I can't differentiate, especially with the girls. I know how it feels to *be* them. Or I think I know how it feels to be them. The counselor says they can't identify their feelings; they don't know if they are "sad" or "angry" or "confused." They don't know how to name it, we have to help them name it, and I think, *I* don't know how to name it.

I am still outside of myself, watching my own life. Watching the girl I was, in the desert smoking pot. Remember her friend? She thought he was her friend but then he is lunging at her, saying to the other boys, I'll show you what else has curves. There are men nearby, across the wide dry riverbed, working construction, the sound of nail guns and hammers, but she screams and when she screams, her voice goes out like a bullet into a tunnel. All other sound stops. What has been close, recedes, what has been far away comes close. She is suddenly invisible, she knows this, how it happens. No one sees her. Her mouth will move, but no one will hear her. They will stand up, walk out of the desert, and she will follow behind. They will talk to one another. If she says something, no one will answer. It's as if what has just happened, has not happened, has been erased. She has been erased. Remember the boy in the trailer when she was six. Remember her mother at the piano. Remember the girl tap dancing on the porch and how the film melts across the screen.

37

My mother is slicing sourdough bread, thin, and spreading it with but-ter and garlic. She is home for lunch; it is our day off. (Last night, our night off. Eight vodka gimlets: two to relax, two to stop worrying about Dina, then four to stop seeing Trish in the cabs with truckers and Angela and her stepfather in the hotel room. I poked my cheek with my fingertip to make sure I was comfortably numb.) Michael and I have come over to my mother's to do laundry. (Where is Fernando? I have no memory. Perhaps gone to his second job or to a class he's taking in social work.) My mother places the bread under the broiler, adds a few leaves of basil from her garden, large slices of tomato, thin slices of white cheese and then under the broiler again until the cheese is just curving down over the tomato, just bubbling from the heat, the bubbles edged brown. I squeeze tangerines for juice, we sit at a card table in the square of light that falls through the sliding-glass door of the family room. (I know, at this moment, that Angela's mother is taking her to a clinic to see about an abortion. It is her stepfather's child but, chances are, the mother won't leave him.) The lawn outside is still greenish, a resident family of quail scurries beneath the orange tree. Michael is lying on his stomach watching cartoons. He wants a chocolate long john. How about cream of wheat? Or a cheese sand-wich? He makes a face. I close my eyes and feel the sun on my back. Contrary to popular opinion, I tell my mother, cheese sandwiches are great for breakfast. (I wonder if she can smell the alcohol oozing from my pores; I wonder if she thinks I am a bad mother.) After we eat, she kisses Michael goodbye and then me, on the forehead, her lip-stick waxy and perfumed. Her heels click across the linoleum. Michael climbs up on my lap and I wrap one arm around him, feel his solid weight against my chest, rest my chin on his head. You smell like a puppy, I tell him.

38

I am upstairs crawling carefully over floorboards old and weathered. Down there, through a sliver of light in the floor, they hold a blanket over Kenny's head, their arms around him, maybe it feels like a caress, he knows, of course he knows, flash of red, that's all. A young girl sits up in bed, turns away from her lover, holds her arms out. Across her breasts dark blue veins, a webbing beneath translucent skin. The house is wood, the house will burn, thick with flame and smoke, Michael's choked sobbing, he can't get a breath and my heart contracts, no, this is a dream.

A dream, and two swans glide. When the girl opens her mouth, round stones rise into the air. I crawl out the window, crouch on green shingles, treetops feathery in rain, the air washed blue by rain. I move as if through cool water, my bones are water, I swim away, off the roof into the air, away. But Michael is downstairs, his face in the window, tears pool in his eyes, swans part the dark water and his arm reaches from the window, his hand grasps my braid, pulling, pulling on my braid, pulling himself to me where I am swimming in the sky, my braid stretched between us.

39

In the evenings, in a low house over on Granada, that's where my poetry class from the community college meets. Maybe it's not a class—they all seem old to me, not like students—maybe it's a group of poets, and the professor has invited me to join. He reads a poem for his brother, his brother a doctor who has been shot by one of his mental patients. Maybe the poem is written in his brother's memory or maybe *to* re-member, literally, *re-member*, to bring back together all the parts of his brother, the long limbs, the easy smile, the quick gestures of his brother in motion. The house is hollow and so the professor's words echo and the air smells slightly of hashish. The floors are wooden, old Persian rugs, carvings from Africa, brass gongs and platters from India. One man wears loose white clothing, a Nehru shirt. The women, even though they are old, in their thirties or forties, maybe, wear their hair long and loose. I expect to see, on any given night, flowers, flowers woven through their hair, gardenias, as if it's still the 60s, as if there's still hope.

40

As if the streets aren't full of lost children. As if I, like their mothers, won't abandon them. As if I will even remember their names: Dina, Veronica, Trish, Sammy, Kenny, Paul, Angela, Curtis (whose older brothers helped his father beat their mother), Rosemary, Gabby, Wendy, Brian, Alma (who loved another girl), Manuela (the girl she loved), JoAnna, Doug, Moira, Todd (who, like Dina, kept coming back), Jeff (who will pull an empty gun on a cop, suicide by police), and then the girl, the Navajo girl, Barbara?, who saw ghosts upstairs and was afraid to fall asleep. And then the others, a hundred others. But I will get pregnant and one of the kids, Jimmy, an eight-year-old pyromaniac, will threaten to kick me in the belly, in the belly, he says, belly, his word, and kill your baby. And I will grab him by his armpits and drag him across the picnic table. Say that again, I tell him, giving him a hard shake and I'll kill you. I mean it. And I know his history, I know his mother is a prostitute and that her boyfriends started blowing pot smoke in his face when he was two, I know the counselor has just taken him off Ritalin, I know the other kids have been teasing him, and still I mean it. With all my heart and gut, with both arms and both hands and my teeth, I mean it. If I were another person, I would divide in two. I would have a life where I could take care of this child, these other children, and then go home and grow basil or something. Clean the kitchen. I would be noble and calm. But I only have the one life and, often, within it, I am not calm or reasonable or understanding. My rage, as I am shaking this child, scares me.

41

I buy a small house from a Mormon woman on the northwest side of town. Far from my parents, far from Fernando's parents, far from the Shelter. I have decided we should become exiles. I am tired, I guess, of being inhabited by others, which is what working with the kids at the Shelter feels like, which is what listening to the troubles about Marty feels like, which is what my parents' declining marriage feels like. All of these people, their sorrows get lodged in me and I cannot dislodge them, not even from my dreams. When I go to the grocery store, as I am testing the tomatoes or avocados, complete strangers tell me their stories. It's as if I have become a magnet, a receptacle, something on my face must invite them. I am not a storyteller, but a story hearer, a sin-eater, and I wish there were some way to transform these details into a poem or a song, into sound pure sound, music, because then I could open my mouth and their sorrows would go out into the air, have a place to vibrate that was *not* inside of me.

42

That first winter, it rains and rains as if we have moved to some foreign place, away from the desert; it rains and it rains, and the water comes up to the back step and I think it will enter the house. It rains and the roof leaks and we poke holes in the ceilings with an ice pick so that the water will come down in a stream and fill the bowls and buckets we've placed in the corners of the rooms. It rains and the ivy that grows up the front of the house begins to grow into the house; it worms its way into the cracks between the window frames and the adobe blocks. The outside is coming inside and I sometimes feel like the adobes will melt and the process will be complete. Nature will reclaim us.

Kathryn is born that winter of the rains, and she cries so much because of colic and ear infections that I enroll Michael in nursery school. I want him to have time and space of his own away from us, away from her crying and my crankiness, and when the teachers remark on what a happy little boy he is, they've never seen such a happy little boy, they say—I can only think that he is happy because he is in school, away from us, away from our unhappy house that rains on the inside, our unhappy house on the street of small square houses with Bermuda grass and big mulberry trees.

This is the house where we'll live when the children are small and I am going to school. In summer, there are peaches on the tree outside of our bedroom window, and the grape vines tumble from the arbor over the fence. Grass grows knee high, so high that the little dog Duke gets lost. Mornings in summer, I fill the plastic swimming pool with water. Michael and Kathryn climb in, pour water from yellow margarine tub to yellow margarine tub. Sunlight makes their hair shine copper, gets caught in the round drops of water that arc through the air. I feel the sun on my back, on my arms and face, smell the beans on the stove in the kitchen behind me, the wet smell of earth in the garden, dark and rich with worms, tomatoes, that acrid smell at the stems, zucchini, the flesh sticky. This is what motherhood gives you, I think, every day a rhythm, a melody, a taproot into the earth.

In the afternoons, in the bedroom with the red curtains, I fall asleep while I'm reading, a child napping on each side of me, I fall into a sleep so deep I feel drugged. I dream of intruders, my eyelids so heavy I cannot open them although I know someone's in the house. Finally, I rise, I walk down the hall, there is someone there, I can feel him although I cannot see him, and the children are behind me, sleeping, defenseless in the room with summer light. My eyelids are so heavy that even as I'm walking, I cannot lift them, so heavy, and then I realize, I have not risen. There is someone in the house. I have to get up. Get up. Get up. Open my eyes. But they are so heavy, as heavy as my limbs in water, as heavy as the peach tree's limbs in summer storms, as heavy as time and memory and the memory of moving through time.

43

There was a ghost in the Modern Languages Building. One of the Spanish professors, an Episcopalian priest, exorcised the whole fifth floor. Spanish and Portuguese, Italian and French, the Romance Languages were haunted, but the bad spirits didn't leave the building. They simply moved downstairs to English. Ask anyone. I was an undergraduate at the time, already twenty-six, two small children at home. But the bad spirits, the ones who moved down to English, had nothing to do with the ghost. The ghost had always been seen in the basement or on the main floor, perhaps in the breezeway at night after poetry readings. Her white gown, she wore a long white gown. She had been raped and murdered long ago, long before the building even stood. Perhaps her body had been buried there in the middle of the desert. Perhaps it had been thrown down a well or into a mining shaft. She'd been alone for a long long time, years, decades, and now she must wonder who all these people are, how they move through her but do not hear.

It takes a great deal of energy to manifest yourself when you're invisible. My voice sounded hollow, hollowed out, when I tried to speak in class. Heart pounding. I was twenty-six; we had two young children; my husband painted houses; I babysat to help out. I had one blue skirt, gauze, no, not gauze, crinkled cotton, in tiers, turquoise and red bric-a-brac at each tier. Two cotton tee shirts: one red, one turquoise. I had one jean skirt, one melon-colored blouse from India. I wore those Chinese straw sandals. I tried to fit in. I watched my feet as I crossed campus. I talked to myself. I said, you, you've had a gun pulled on you, you've done really stupid crazy things, you've given birth twice, so how can simply speaking terrify you? Simply hearing your voice in a room full of strangers? Or sometimes I said: did you hear her today? She understood all the assumptions the professor listed on the board; she understood how those assumptions colored the reading of *Ulysses*; she understood why Molly said *yes* or why, rather, Joyce could say yes *only* through Molly. This was her thesis. She understood Molly.

She learned how to put parentheses around parts of words to suggest hidden or paradoxical meanings. It was a kind of typography, a secret language, modern hieroglyphics. She liked the way it looked on the page. She understood semiotics. She understood a tree was a *sign* while a Christmas tree was a *symbol*. (However, a tree could *also* be a symbol, couldn't it? As in that Yeats poem? Plath's yew tree? Didn't it depend upon context or other textual features? But she wasn't brave enough to ask.) She understood that words always referred to something else. Words were like desire in that desire was always deferred. The object of desire, always unobtainable. Life, therefore, the state of longing.

44

The little white girl with her cotton candy hair is standing at the front screen in her nightgown. It is ten o'clock. The news is on. Hey-elp! my uncle is trying to shoot my daddy! I open the screen and let her in. There is noise from next door. Loud voices. They are from Florida. The people from Texas, on the other side, shoot their guns, too, but mostly on New Years, Fourth of July. A Southern tradition? I ask Fernando, some alternative form of firecrackers? But they've begun to do it in L.A., too, only with semiautomatics. If you're out at midnight, stand under a concrete overpass. Bullets fall. Bullets rain down.

According to the little girl, bullets are getting lodged in the dining room ceiling and have broken a lamp. Fernando stands up. Oh, no, I tell him, her uncle would as soon shoot you as look at you. This is not theoretical. They do not allow our children in their house. Their children are allowed in our house but they have been instructed not to use the bathrooms. Mexicans are dirty, the little girl tells me. That's why.

Bullets fall with great speed, something to do with mass, density, and the force of gravity. Someone could do an equation, I'm sure, and calculate the trajectory of death. But here's another equation for you: white dude is mad at his brother, white dude has a gun, brown dude enters the house.

The little girl with the cotton candy hair starts crying harder. We call the cops. Her face, usually pinched and white, is now mottled pink. *Mochos* run out of her nose. She wipes at it with her fist. She is ugly and weak, this little girl, who will come over, uninvited, open our refrigerator and look for food, who will eat our cookies and drink our milk but not use the toilets because we are dirty. She will show up at night, expecting help, her voice, like her plump mother's, soft, southern, sibilant, all diphthongs and honey.

45

Fernando dreams about a brick wall, a revolver on a window ledge, and birds. He dreams he is in prison. It's very early in the morning, the sun just lightening the walls. I should have gone instead of Marty, Fernando says, he *always* says. Sshh, I say. It doesn't matter that this makes no sense; he believes it, that he could, somehow, have taken his brother's place. Suffered for him. And that, because he didn't, he failed him. I don't understand it, am often impatient with what I see as a kind of free-floating Catholic guilt. But I kiss his neck. Because arguments get us nowhere, I run my open hand first over his chest and then under the waistband of his underwear, back and forth over the hair just beneath his belly button. Ssshhh, I croon, sshh. As if I think desire can change everything.

In prison, Fernando whispers, Marty had to do what the lieutenants told him. If they said get me a shank, run this dope, pass that piece, he had to do it. If they told him, go get the ring off that guy, lean on him, put a snitch jacket out on him, I want him for my *puta*, Marty had to do it.

Fernando sighs. He is lying with his arm across his eyes. Marty was sitting out by the phones, he says, and this little Mexican dude was on the phone. Everything's cool, well, until this big white guy comes and yanks the Mexican off the phone, pushes him to the ground, and then starts using the phone himself. So they're all sitting there and pretty soon, the Mexican guy, he's this little shit, *mean*, he comes back, he has this sharpened piece of rebar and he shoves it through the guy's back. While he's on the phone. He shoves it so hard, it comes out the front of him. And so I asked him, I said, God, Marty, didn't you see the guy coming? And he said, what the fuck, if I'd warned the white guy, the Mexican guy's friends would've been on me. Just like if I'd warned the Mexican in the first place, the white guys would've beaten the shit out of me. The phones were right by this classroom and when the teacher heard everything, he opened the door but when he saw the white dude lying there with the rebar through him, he just shut the door and locked it. And so I thought, fuck, if the teacher won't do nothing, I'd better not.

Fernando is staring at the ceiling, trying to understand it, how Marty could remain silent against everything inside himself. The white dude is lying there, choking on his own blood, and his brother is doing nothing.

It's a different world in there, I tell him. We can't judge what he did in there by how we live out here. This is what I say, what I keep telling him, keep telling myself, but it provides no consolation, no understanding of what it must be like to live in a cement square, no wind, no human touch, no vulnerability, no one to listen. A different world. Just look at Danny Lyon's photographs, the male bodies honed and decorated like instruments of destruction. We can't take our eyes off their tattoos. The visiting room may smell like the zoo, but it's a war zone. Don't kid yourself. Long stretches of boredom punctuated by extreme violence, violence meant not to kill, but to maim, mutilate, terrify. Like the little Mexican guy said: that'll teach you to fuck with me.

This is not to say I feel only compassion for Marty. I don't. I preferred it when he was in prison, when Fernando wasn't drinking away his guilt, when we didn't have to worry about what Marty might do, what he might steal, how he might bring trouble down on the family. That time a car pulled up next to his sister's at a red light and the guy shoved a shotgun in her window. *Tell your brother we want our money.* There were children in the backseat.

Fear is a hard seed next to my heart. I don't want my life invaded by the violence in Marty's. He is the past incarnate, a past I've tried to leave behind, a past I don't want to touch my children. I tell my children not to open the door if they're home alone and he knocks. In a few years, after his second stint, I will turn him in to his parole officer and he will get sent back for the rest of his sentence. There are many days when I would feel a kind of relief if he were found dead in an alley. I should just confess it: I am not as good, not as forgiving as Fernando.

46

In God's eyes, all sins are the same. A lie weighs the same as murder. This is the gospel according to Marty. Later, years later, no, decades later, we will find out he's heard voices since he was eighteen, in prison the first time, first just God's, then the demon's, then a continuous radio broadcast, voices that never stop, a whispering of sins past and future, a quarreling of voices, cops down the street tuning in, say, or addicts upstairs, three apartments over, plotting to kill him. Marty has a heightened sense of hearing, can tune in but cannot tune out. Trauma triggered the voices; heroin quiets them. But his anguish is this: if he believed enough, if he was worthy, then God would help him.

47

From the open end of the courtyard to the old adobe chapel and back, the dancers march in the midday sun. It is the day before Easter in Old Pascua. When Fernando was little, his father brought him to the dances, and now we bring the children. Half of the dancers wear black pants and shirts, black hoods over their heads; the other half, the *chapayekas*, wear costumes of serapes, animal masks over their faces, geometrical eyes, long fangs. What they wear represents evil. One wears the mask of a white man, stethoscope around his neck, black bag in his hand. One wears a Burger King crown. Back and forth they dance in the sweltering sun, beneath airless masks, their bare feet in rhythm. They have been fasting all week, all of them. They have made a *manda*, a promise, and they dance so their prayers will be answered. They hold crucifixes in their mouths so the evil won't enter their bodies.

The medieval priests herd the *chapayekas* back and forth, whipping them to keep them from entering the chapel. The priests, in black robes and hoods, remind me of old drawings in history books, of processions in Spain, the Inquisition. They are the ones who look evil. Maybe the dance is a joke the Yaquis played on the priests who would convert them. What are they called again, I ask Fernando, the ones who look like priests? *Pharisees*, he says. He is tall, like his father, Spanish-looking, but the dancers are his cousins and he is thinking about sacrifice. He is thinking about Marty, how he has just been released from prison, how he needs to make a *manda*.

Fernando, like his father, holds himself like a *hacendado*, but his mother is small, her skin dark, and so she was called "*prieta*" when she was a child. She remembers the other children taunting her. "*Prieta!*" "*India!*" On the way home from school, they threw small stones at her and laughed. She faced them, stomped her foot, and then she crossed the street into this neighborhood where the Yaquis lived and entered her *Tía's* home. *Tu familia*, Fernando's father still teases her, *puro indios*.

Pharisees, Fernando says. Hypocrites. The self-righteous. What does it matter if your house is clean if your heart is black? Marty has just been released from prison. *Mándame*, Fernando prays, dear Lord, tell me what to do to help him stay straight. Fernando is his brother's keeper, or wants to be, but I say Marty has to make his own promises.

High noon and the bleachers are full of tourists. The people from the neighborhood, the families of the dancers, stand shoulder to shoulder. In the very front row, the *abuelas* sit in lawn chairs. Michael and Kathryn are sitting down front with Fernando's *Tía* Shorty. The dancers are moving faster and faster, their feet in the rising dust. The old women fan themselves. Little girls in white communion dresses are being led through the dancers by their *ninos*, they whip the dancers with sticks wound in bright crepe paper. When the children reach the opening of the chapel, they turn to defend it. The animal spirits storm the chapel two times and, each time, the little girls throw confetti, brightly colored confetti, streams of tiny flowers fall on the dancers and repel them.

Now the bell is ringing, now is the third time, and the animal dancers are victorious, they enter the chapel, and when they emerge, they are bare-chested, wearing only shorts. They are carrying a large papier mâché Judas. They must run and burn Judas in effigy, they must run back and get their own animal masks and costumes and feed the fire. The bell is ringing and ringing and they run faster and faster in the dust and heat, in their thirst and hunger. Some of them stumble, some are falling, they are old or weak, they need help, and people run to help them. They must burn everything evil before the bell stops ringing. The bonfire rises as they feed it, hallucinatory, Judas its dark human center. The crowd, drawn by the flames, breaks up. A man leaning in the shade on the porch, a *tecato*, has that sucked-out look old junkies get.

Fernando is afraid for his brother. He can't remember a time when Marty was not a part of his life. *Mándame*. Tell me what to do. But who has that kind of faith? To give your will over to a God who allowed the Inquisition and the Holocaust? *Mándame*. Fernando is steadfast, but my faith is a stream of confetti flowers, dust motes in a shaft of light. Breath and heartbeat. Michael and Kathryn. Where are they? They are standing, over there, in line for snow cones. Raspberry is blue.

48

Easter Eve in New Pascua the deer will dance. We'll walk through the dark parking lot toward the lights, past old men lying in the shadows, past young men leaning in the shadows, still drinking and laughing, and stand next to a young couple, both of them with long hair, his arms wrapped around her, chin resting on her head. The old men of the tribe will sit in a line on the edge of the ramada playing their instruments, gourds in water, drums made of animal skin, and the deer will dance over to them, paw the ground, slowly dancing, slowly, his bare feet in the dust. The dancer has the head of a deer strapped on top of his own head and we will forget he is human, see instead the face of the deer, the eyes of the deer, its eyes, as it dances slowly. The deer will tilt his head, he will listen, his eyes dark and wary, ears alert. When he is still, he is testing the wind, testing for danger.

In the deer dance, the deer is the symbol of Christ. The coyotes stalk him, circling and circling, until finally they kill him. Until then, the coyotes are tricksters, they make lewd gestures when they dance, poke each other in the butt, stagger as if they are drunk, make loud noises. They are the ones we enjoy watching. We watch the deer quietly, reverently, but then the coyotes come forward and we wait because the coyotes play tricks on us, too, they fill their mouths with water and rush out into the people, spitting water in long arcs everywhere, chasing each other out into the shadows away from the light of the ramada until young boys chase them back to the dance.

It seems sad to me that we love the one who is going to die. Maybe we love him because we know he is going to die, maybe because we're told he dies for us. But we also love the coyotes, the tricksters who will kill him, who charm us before they do it. Until that moment, the coyotes will dance around the deer, circling and circling, and we will listen. The sound of the drum is the sound of the deer's heartbeat, the sound of the shells, his breathing. We, too, will breathe with the deer, with the rhythm of the shells, the rhythm of the earth, our hearts will beat in rhythm with his, and yet we'll watch as the coyotes stalk him. There is nothing we can do about it. We know they will kill him right before dawn.

49

If Michael and Kathryn were to stand before the front window of the house of their childhood and place their cupped palms on either side of their eyes, they would see their father walk into the kitchen after work with his brothers. All of them tall men, they will pull back chairs and drink beer, laugh, tell stories about the cat who came up through the hole in the floor. It sat on their father's chest, they will say, like the devil one night, trying to steal his breath away from him. As Michael and Kathryn watch, their mother will pour salsa into cottage cheese and put potato chips on the table or guacamole with corn chips. She will stir in a little cottage cheese, to stretch the avocado, which is expensive. They know they will get to stay up late that night, listening. It will be almost as good as Christmas Eve at Nana's house or as a summer barbecue at Aunt Terri's, only without all their cousins running around, only without Nana checking on the tamales or holding a baby. Without their aunts adding details to the stories, making salsa, grinding, in the stone *molcajete*, the little red chilies that make your eyes water. They will get to stay up late and listen, but tonight it will be a night without their Tata's Spanish.

At Grandma's house, it is different. There is an inside voice and an outside voice. If your hands are clean and you promise not to pound, you can play the baby grand piano in the room with the pale blue carpet and old furniture. At Christmas you can help Grandma put the gingerbread house together with white frosting. In summer you can watch Grandpa teeter on the edge of the diving board as he shows you how to do a back dive. His feet are very white and his toenails are yellow. His glass of whiskey and ice and coke sits sweating near the steps at the shallow end. His antifreeze, he calls it. You can deck dive under him and if you bump him, he stands up, water dripping off his bushy eyebrows, and says, now where did that dolphin go? You have to shout "side" so he won't bump his head on the ladder.

Later, when Michael and Kathryn are old and dream of the house on La Osa, the living room may seem diminished by time, the furniture shabby. They'll see their mother studying, typing at the kitchen table, dishes piled dirty in the sink and stacks of books and papers everywhere. Maybe they'll feel neglected. Maybe they'll see themselves streaming in and out of the kitchen door with their friends, the Ortega brothers, while their mother, oblivious, sits at the kitchen table clicking out words on the typewriter. They'll see themselves digging for treasure in the backyard, trolling the alleys looking for planks of wood to make forts. Kathryn will see herself placing the palms of her hands on her mother's cheeks, turning her mother's face to her own, saying, I'm here, Mom, right here. Standing before you. *Listen.*

Part Three. Notes on Art

*But poems are like dreams: in them you put
what you don't know you know.*
—Adrienne Rich, "When We Dead Awaken:
Writing as Re-Vision"

I

Thirty degrees centigrade. In London, this is hot. It's 2006, a summer of record heat, the air is thick and still. Kathryn and I have stopped over for a few days on our way home from Prague where, for three weeks, we have been at a conference for writers and photographers. Every morning, workshops; every evening, smoky readings or foreign films. She spent her afternoons in darkrooms, I spent mine in cafés with poets or on the balcony, reading manuscripts. Now we are walking along a street with traffic in Bloomsbury, perhaps we are nearing Tottenham Court Road, the fumes heady, the crowds of people slightly overwhelming—no, for Kathryn, absolutely overwhelming. Her anxiety is a fishing line, taut between us. I want her to love London. Instead, she is already speeding toward the future moment when she is going to tell her husband she wants to leave him. We turn away from the crowds, go down a side street, find a small café with tables out front.

Inside, the café is not a café but a health food store with a counter where there are bins of salads and where they will put fruit into a machine and juice will come out. We have places like these at home. Exorbitant. I hold my hand out with the coins whose denominations I do not remember. Without my glasses, I am like a child or Blanche Dubois, dependent upon the kindness of strangers. The young black man with the Rastafarian hair laughs. Oh, he says, the java must be for you.

Outside, at a small round table, the wind comes up or maybe it is the swish of passing cars and we mistake it for wind. A young beggar approaches the table behind us, then ours. He is, I remember, wearing some kind of long heavy coat, conspicuous in the heat. His words have hard edges but sound swallowed. I give him a few fat coins and on his face an expression I recognize. Contempt. It means he could hurt us without compunction. It isn't often you see that on the face of a stranger. Maybe on the face of a lover, you've seen it, just before you realize you must leave him.

I want Kathryn to love London as I do and so I lead her toward King's Cross, toward the neighborhood where I stayed when I was eighteen. Here, I want to show her, here is where I started to become myself; where, when I saw my reflection in a window, I realized I was a separate person, free to invent my own life; where I knew, somehow, that the past does not determine the future.

We are standing on the corner near Russell Square Station where just last summer, one of the bombs went off. I can see the small grocery. The phone booth, the row of apartments with glass balconies that pyramid down to the ground floor. We walk farther. The row houses curve. People around us are not wearing business suits. They push babies in strollers, pull little carts of groceries or laundry. Everything is becoming slightly shabby. We stop in front of a row house, like its neighbors, painted white. There are flower boxes with geraniums. A sign promises a full Irish breakfast. A man with a turban, a Sikh, comes out of the front door.

If we walk any farther, four steps, maybe five, we will see the Indian restaurant where I ate with Richard, the little hardware store, then, in another block or so, Cartwright Gardens and the Avalon Hotel at the end of the crescent. Further down the street, the pub where the Scottish students hung out. We will step into 1972.

But it is my past. Kathryn cannot go with me. She doesn't want to. And I don't want her to. This sudden realization is curious. Unspoken. But we both feel it. We stop walking and stand next to one another, trying to get our bearings. The wind lifts a strand of her long hair and it brushes against my bare shoulder. In few days, I will return home to take care of my mother. Kathryn will ask for a divorce. We both know this. I want to stroke her cheek with my hand and tell her everything will be all right.

2

When I imagined the conference in Prague, I had imagined this: lying on a bed with Kathryn. She would put her head on my shoulder, she would play with my hand like she had done when she was little, turning my wedding band around and around, and when she talked, she would tell me everything. She would tell me why she wanted to leave her husband, she would tell me why there hadn't been any joy in her voice for months. I didn't imagine the famous writers and photographers, the workshops, the readings, the films, the museums. I didn't imagine sitting in a café in the afternoons. I didn't imagine our small apartment, the white gauze curtains billowing in a breeze. I didn't imagine the Charles Bridge, the cobblestone streets, or the surreal blue sky. I didn't imagine the Astronomical Clock or even the towers of the Týn Church. I didn't imagine the castle on the hill. I imagined time with Kathryn.

3

The flash of blue through the leaves of the privet announced Kathryn's boyfriend. Boyfriend? She was fourteen. It was 1992. What I remember now, above all, is regret, is the heaviness of indecision, the inability to draw lines. It was like living in the hottest of summers. As you stood in front of the sink to do dishes, sweat ran down the backs of your legs but you thought maybe it was insects, a line of sugar ants. The inability to tell inside from outside. A heaviness. A paralysis. I was depressed. I was not a good mother. I could not say *no*. I was disoriented. I could only watch.

The whirring of the fan, that's what I remember. Fernando giving himself injections of Interferon, an experimental medicine that will not work. In the afternoons, after working all day in the sun, he lies on the bed sweating. This is what has thrown me off balance, out of kilter. It's as if the world has shifted on its axis, as if gravity might fail and airplanes fall out of the sky. I cannot write. When I drive down the freeway to the community college where I teach a 7:30 a.m. class to thirty people who were not good students in high school, Sinead O'Connor is singing *nothing compares to you*. Tears sting my eyes. I imagine eating alone in a restaurant. Ernesto, one of my students, tells me his father went *like that*. Snap of the fingers. Liver cancer. Someday I will be a widow. Chances are.

4

Fernando and I dream the same dream on the same night—this time about lions, a picket fence. The terrain around us is primordial, jagged mountains thrust up from a violent movement of the earth beneath, canyons and passes we can't navigate, thick forests still steaming with the mists of creation, a creation that seems, somehow, apocalyptic. The world we know no longer exists. In the middle of this, a quiet meadow. Pastoral. Kathryn in my arms, a baby again, and Michael, so small but skipping ahead as if it's not the end of the world at all. There, in the tall grass, lions crouch. Oddly, this is not alarming. The lions are not roaring, not hungry, not hunting, no, they are metaphors—even as we dream I realize this—metaphors of future danger, of how the world can come crashing down, tragedy can tear us asunder. As with the claws of a lion.

When do we have this dream? After we've moved back to the desert, I'm sure. I can see the morning light through the red curtains, hear the sound of doves. But how old are the children? Fernando, in the kitchen, calls out the menu: bagels, blueberry waffles, plain waffles, French toast. If it goes in the toaster, he can make it. Kathryn comes into the room and searches through my drawer for socks. Night recedes. I have to make the deposit, pay the lights, find the essay by Baldwin, make copies for my students. *Sorrow wears us.* Fernando's diagnosis is chronic hepatitis, his liver damaged. No more beer, says the doctor, we want to keep you around for a while.

It is 1990 or '91, then, this diagnosis, the first time we've heard the words chronic hepatitis. We knew he'd had non-A, non-B when he was 20, turned yellow, and nearly died. (This was just before we started dating.) But *non*-A, *non*-B: didn't that sound as if what he had wasn't real, did not exist? But it did, and it had for almost twenty years been swimming in his blood stream. In 1990, he would have been thirty-eight. I was in my mid-thirties. I tried to imagine being a widow. It seemed impossible. *If you spend your entire life in flight from death, you are also in flight from life.* Things change and they never change. Fernando's liver was not well. The past was intruding upon the present, or maybe the past simply dwells within the present in the way that cells exist within the body, errant cells tick tick ticking, and still, the coo of the dove, the children argue, there is cacophony, chaos, entropy.

Fernando, his dark hair short and curling at the nape of his neck, comes into the room to make sure I'm awake and soon I will rise and shower and go down to drink the coffee he's made. The yellow school bus will fill the front window; the children will shut the door behind them. The dogs will chase one another around and around the backyard, their sleek tawny bodies leaping like deer. Fernando will read to me from the morning paper and I'll nod, half-listening, making blue marks on a yellow pad of paper for class. Baldwin. Things I must not neglect to say. *You can't know anything about life and suppose you can get through it clean.*

5

In 1986 we moved back to the desert, back after graduate school, back from California, the land of golden dreams and golden dreamers. I had been one of them, thought graduate school would solve all of our problems. To get there, we had driven miles, thousands of miles, it seemed, through the Arizona desert, north through L.A. traffic with a U-Haul trailer swaying precariously on the back of our old car, the other cars whizzing by us, cutting us off, the U-joint going out on a mountain pass, Fernando lying under the car in a parking lot, and then farther north, up the long California coast, to another parking lot in front of a green stucco apartment building. Married student housing, our home for two years, and the desk was upstairs. What was the desk doing upstairs? In the children's room? How would I write? Where would I study? Where would their beds go? I could hear my voice rising and rising. It was a huge, heavy desk, dark wood, hard wood, walnut maybe, as heavy as my father's desk at home, and the stairway was narrow and steep. Fernando jerked the drawers out, picked up one end of the desk and started jerking it across the floor. It's okay, I said. Never mind, I said. We don't have to move it now, I said. But I knew to pick up the other end. I had hit some nerve inside of him that he would never talk about. The nerve was this: my panic over never having time to write was a snake strangling his heart. It meant he couldn't provide well enough. That's what he thought I meant. If you made more money, I would have time to write. That's what he thought I meant. And so we dragged the desk to the top of the stairs. He was on the downstairs side, I was trying to hang on with my fingertips, the children, standing behind me, were quiet. Absolutely quiet. In the face of Fernando's sudden anger, we all knew to say nothing. There was nothing to say. The desk must be moved. Now. And there were no brothers to call. No family to rely on. We had no jobs. The graduate fellowship covered only tuition. We had no jobs. We had saved one thousand dollars and the rent for one month was five hundred and if the desk slipped, it would push him down the stairs and pin him to the wall. What have I *done*, I wanted to wail, bringing us here? What was I thinking?

6

Uncorking the bottle in the middle of the afternoon seemed oh, so, Jean Rhys. If only I had some absinthe. Some pernod. I needed to go to the thrift shop on California Street where rich women donated their clothes so I could buy some nice black jeans, maybe some chinos, a few sweaters. A silk scarf, maybe that would do it. Shoes. I needed shoes that didn't look like they came from K-Mart. Two women from workshop had actually asked me if I got my shoes at K-Mart—not that *I* had anything in particular against K-Mart except that their tee shirts never held their shape after a few washings.

But I got the picture. I was in need of transformation. Evidently so was my story. One woman had asked, why can't you ever write about independent women? Women who *don't* have children? Another student described the story as "about a spiritual crisis—but in the domestic sphere." This, to him, was out of kilter. The spiritual and the domestic did not belong in the same story. The professor agreed. The husband, he said, is a phone number on the wall. Interesting. It could be interesting. A sign of suburban alienation? Bourgeois angst?

A sign of suburban alienation? What suburbs? You could hardly call La Osa, with the Texans and Floridians shooting their guns and the old man down the street mowing his lawn in his Speedo and cowboy boots, the suburbs. How had this happened? How had they misread me so completely? But of course the husband in the story was a phone number on the wall. In the world of the story, they assumed, perhaps I assumed, everyone was white, but I didn't know how to write about a white husband and so the husband disappeared from the story completely. Or, in the world of the story, everyone was Mexican. I'd written one "about" Johnny and Lupe: Fernando's drinking funneled into Johnny, Lupe's anger and helplessness, my own. "El Perdito" was about a little lost Mexican boy who rides his tricycle down the freeway at night. I didn't know how to meld the worlds; in every novel I'd read, they were separate. Art might imitate life, but even in Leslie Silko's *Ceremony*, Tayo, the half-breed, is torn between worlds, has to choose one.

If the literature you read, Renato Rosaldo has said, does not reflect your experiences, it's as if you do not exist. Precisely. And yet we did exist, Fernando and the children and me, we were shape-shifters: we could go back and forth at will, fluent in both cultures, speaking both languages, if only metaphorically. In the house, in our home, we created our own world, separate from the outside, a space in between. Where we came from mostly didn't matter. But when there were conflicts, they were too complicated, too private, too close to the bone. First person terrified me. Even using the disclaimer of fiction, there were too many layers of possible betrayal. Anyway, no one would believe it.

I opened the red wine. Called my friend back in Tucson. She said, tell them the novel is a bourgeois art form. Oh, I thought—I did not say it, not even to her—oh, I would *love* to be a member of the bourgeoisie, even the petite bourgeoisie. I *aspire* to be a member of the bourgeoisie. Being a member of the noble proletariat requires far too much self-denial and I don't have the opiate of religion.

No, but I had red wine. Cheap red wine from France and I was chugging it straight from the bottle. Kathryn was pulling on my sleeve. Oh, Mom, she said, why do you listen to *them*? What do *they* know?

Kathryn wanted me to be a mom, not a writer. She wanted me to follow her outside to the central grassy area where precisely at five p.m. the sprinklers would come on. At each sprinkler, a boy was crouched, waiting for the burst of water so he could aim the rain-birds at the other boys. It was war. Kathryn wanted her turn.

Such were the days of graduate school with young children. The noise, the chaos, the feverishness and delight. The days when all you wanted to do was stop time and gaze upon them. Memorize them. The days when your patience was cracked thin and there was still dinner to make, baths to run, stories to tell, papers to grade, dishes to wash, papers to write, sex with your husband (sex, what was that?)—and all before you could sit down and read 200 pages of Derrida who used the Preface to Retrieve his Seed.

7

How big do you think Israel is? Rivka, the biologist from Israel asks. (I have no idea.) As big as the Bay area, she tells me, but we seem bigger because we make such a noise in the world. Only seven miles across at the smallest point. The Six Day War, had I heard of it? (No.) Her husband, Moshe, had fought in it, as well as the Yom Kippur War. Moshe strokes my cheek with the back of his hand in greeting. And you, Rivka asks Fernando, what are you? Mexican, he says. Oh, no, she says, you are not Mexican. I met some Mexicans the other night. You are American. Maybe you are, partly, a Jew? You look like a Jew. (This was possible, of course: his father looked just like the photographs of Frida Kahlo's father; his father's mother had emigrated as a child from Germany to Mexico.) *Maybe*, Fernando agrees. (Later he shrugs, *probably*: blood knows blood.) Married Student Housing. The fall picnic. We are standing in front of the salads. *Cre-a-tive Wri-ting?* the Japanese doctoral student in engineering asks me, spooning rice onto his paper plate, *what is this? Cre-a-tive Wri-ting?* And your husband, what does he study? Oh, my husband is the spouse. Your husband is the spouse? Thanks, Fernando says, I'm The Spouse. Well, I say, you have the Spouse Card. I have the Student Card. And this is Kevin, Kathryn's little friend from Guatemala, his parents are studying medicine. Soon they will take Kevin and his brother home, where they will go to the mountain villages and inoculate indigenous people. But we can stay in each village for only a few days, the father tells Fernando in Spanish, because if the soldiers find out we are there, they will come. The father from Colombia will not allow his son, even though he is older than Michael, in the fifth grade, to walk to and from school with the other children. It is quite safe, I tell him. Yes, he says, but he must not get used to such freedoms. The woman from Pakistan misses her mother. She wears beautiful saris but her daughter wears pants and climbs the gnarled pepper tree that shades the sandbox. The wives from Japan don't want to go home. Here, they can drive cars and play golf. Too expensive in Japan. Hans, the chemistry professor from Switzerland, worries about the grad students, they have cots next to their desks so they can sleep close to their experiments, they never go home to their families. His wife, Doris, is a photographer and we sometimes drink tea in the afternoons. Earl Gray. Bergamot. I love the lilt in Doris's voice, the way she presses the back of her hand to my cheek in greeting. We ride our bikes through the green hills, along the top where we can see all the way to San Francisco. Oh, the French scholar says to me, gesticulating wildly, Creative Writing! Only in America! The novel, he says, is dead. In France, everyone has written one. I myself have written five. They are in my desk drawer. Did you know, asks his wife, who studied literature at the Sorbonne, when they cut open schizophrenics on the operating table, they find in their stomachs, pens?

8

My mother said, tell the children not to break anything. Those plates, the blue and white ones in the dining room, are museum pieces. Tell them not to throw anything in the house. (As if I needed to tell my children *not* to throw objects in another person's home. Let's not shove peas up our noses, I might as well say, let's not cut one another with knives.) Aunt Dorothy and Uncle Charles. Their house was up in the valley, built in three wings and so made an angular U, a cove, in the center of which was a pool such as I had never seen before, painted black or dark blue and, as I remember, there were water lilies, plants cascading down to the water. Michael and Kathryn loved to play there by the pool, catching water skippers. We would sit inside in the library, watching them through the glass doors, drinking vermouth with a twist of lemon before lunch.

Dorothy said she could watch them for hours. Charles and Fernando walked around the house and looked at the watercolors Charles's uncle had painted at the turn of the century. They were beautiful. Some were detailed with the precise hand of a botanist, others were impressionistic. London, a wash of gray with the thinnest of lines for definition. Incredible blues, the Cerulean blues of Greece and Spain, the lush greens of the South Seas. The Taj Mahal, a bluish dome, wavering in the distance. Fernando's face, relaxed as he listens to Charles. I realize this may be the first time he has ever felt completely at ease with my family.

Dorothy, in those days, a woman in dark glasses, wearing a Katharine Hepburn hat and trousers and a high-necked blouse, a woman sitting in the middle of her masterpiece, her beautiful garden, next to a dark pool, surrounded by lemon trees in their black pots, waxy green ferns, fragrant narcissus. When I loaned her a journal of feminist essays to read, she said, what a luxury to worry about your name, what you call yourself, instead of how you're going to feed your children. This reminded me, of course, of Virginia Woolf, *A Room of One's Own*, her consciousness of the women cleaning kitchens, taking care of other women's children, while she had the luxury of setting words to paper. Virginia Woolf, who would have been only eighteen the year Dorothy was born, who would not publish until Dorothy was in her twenties, old enough to buy her books. Years later, when Dorothy told me the story of her father waiting for her mother to die, this memory would make a different kind of sense. Oh, I thought then, no wonder Dorothy had no conflict over last names and chose Charles's over her own, over her father's. Charles was a gentle and kind man.

The straw picnic basket was huge, lined with checked blue fabric. Often, Dorothy packed it with baguettes and sliced turkey, some salami, a bottle of chilled white wine from Washington, apples, cheese. Charles placed it the trunk of their old Mercedes, 1965, maybe older, and we climbed in, Charles driving, Michael and Fernando next to him in the front seat, Kathryn between Dorothy and me in the back. Kathryn always slipped one hand into Dorothy's and one into mine. Dorothy wore very dark wraparound sunglasses whenever she went outside, and Kathryn would put her nose right up against Dorothy's to see if she could see her eyes. This was while we were nestled in the backseat of the car on our way to Point Lobo, where we would unpack the straw basket at a picnic table under the cypress trees. Later, our picnics would take place on the gray sand of Carmel Beach, so we could wheel Charles's chair as close to the water as possible. Still later, Charles's and Dorothy's ashes would be spread there, over the gray ocean, off the point.

9

The avenue is shady and there are booths set up and we buy wine glasses and wander from booth to booth and taste the wine, half a glass of glimmering wine. Cheers! To my master's thesis! A thin red book with gold lettering on its spine, bound like a real book, it will reside in Green Library in the stacks along with all the other books, not in the basement where the pipes leak and the pages swell, where I found Fielding's *Pamela*, old and musty, printed so long ago the letter "s" looked like a feathery "f" and so it seemed, when I was tired, reading late at night, as if Fielding had had a lisp. ("I ♥ the eighteenth century," all the handouts from the professor had said.) Sauvignon blanc from the valley we have never seen and so it still seems golden. We lift our sunny glasses. It is a summer day and the children want to go to the creamery where they can pick out candies and someone will mash the candies into ice cream and then spoon the ice cream into a real waffle which has been shaped into a cone. Only in California! This is California, a place where there are coffee shops tucked into the corner of bookstores, where there is a rack of newspapers from all over the world, where lines are long and you hear languages other than English and Spanish. A place where the illegals Fernando works with are from New Zealand and Australia and Wales; where, when the *Migra* comes on the job, they go directly to Fernando and where, later at the bar, the guys say, *Oh, Mate, as long as we don't open our mouths* . . . This is California where on Sundays we drive over the coastal mountains on a windy road down to San Gregorio Beach. California, where succulents bloom on the edges of sandy cliffs and mornings are gray with fog, where Fernando and I pull huge branches of driftwood together, hang sheets and beach towels to make a shelter from the wind and, while the children play there in the sand, we watch the clouds turn white, then the line of silver along the horizon, which is the sunlight, then the ocean as it turns a bluer gray. California where, on the very first afternoon, we'd pulled the drawers out of the heavy desk and I could barely hold on, where we'd placed the desk below the window in the dining room. California where every night, after Fernando and the children were asleep, I could drink my red wine and do research and write my papers; where every morning, while the children were in school, I could work on my stories. California where I could gaze out the window at the Japanese plum trees, their leaves purplish red. In spring they would blossom; in an earthquake they would sway.

10

My father could speak dog, which is to say on Sunday afternoons, after a few drinks, the kids would beg him to howl. Sunday dinner at my mother's, not the good silver, but manners, yes, mind your manners. This is back in Tucson, after our California sojourn. We've moved back into our small house on the small street, the Floridians and Texans on either side. We tear out carpeting, lay tile, paint the walls and cabinets. Make everything ours again. Still it feels like failure, in a way, to come back. To what? Teaching a few classes at the community college, tutoring at the university. Fernando, starting a business with his brothers. There is family here. This is why we've come back. Home. Home is both refuge and trap. On Sundays, my father takes his ice cream bowl behind the corner and licks it clean. Please, the children beg him, please, and he climbs on the diving board and sets the neighbors' dogs to barking. My mother could speak dog, too, but her yips were usually of disapproval. Why do you let Kathryn wear red lipstick? She looks like a streetwalker. Why do you let her play basketball with boys? Because she's *that* good. But why with black boys and Mexican boys? Michael plays with blacks and Mexicans. It's not the same, she says. Michael and Kathryn *are* Mexican, Mom. *You know what I mean.* But to be fair, she lets Kathryn bring friends over to swim. Black girls in the pool, of whatever shade, are not as threatening as black boys. Michael never asks if his friends can come. He knows better. Kathryn pushes it. Don't go darker than your father, my mother will say to her later, when she's in college, he's a nice shade of brown.

I I

The skinny girls with their new breasts stream in and out, always aligning and realigning their personal allegiances. Who is queen for the day? Café au lait, mocha, freckled, these are the colors of their skin. Mixed marriages are common in our neighborhood. Green eyes, hair in ponytails, regal, bitchy, as only thirteen-year-olds can be. They glue condoms in colored wrappers to their posters for health class. They giggle, are merciless gossips, delight in being mean. We live in the house of the multitudes. Teenage boys sprawl in front of the TV playing Nintendo, their long legs taking up the whole living room floor. The sound of Mario Brothers invades even my sleep. Boing! Boing! Boing! Where oh where is the princess? Step over the boys' long long legs to get to the kitchen but don't expect any clean dishes. In my bedroom, I move the pile of clothes off the bed onto the desk so we can sleep at night; during the day, I lift the pile back onto the bed so I can use the computer. This is in the room with red curtains, the peach tree outside the window, the fan whirring day and night to drown out the noise of the multitudes, their chomping on food like insects, as if the house is full of termites and soon the walls will crumble around us.

I 2

In my friend's tiny apartment, the bedroom is the living room, the dining room is the office. Her computer resides on a small table under a tablecloth. Take it off, voila! A workspace. While she's in Aix en Provence, I try on her life: teapot on tiny stove, buttery crackers no one has to share, books books books, original art by friends, plants that need water. (Susan has time to water plants?) On the bookshelves, in bound leather, her journals, one for every year of her life since she learned to write. Her life recorded, her own private fiction, but it seems dangerous to me, those words, there, where anyone could step into her apartment and read them.

I have autobiography anxiety. I remember the first time I felt it. I was reading the journal I'd kept all through junior high, we were moving from Grand Junction, and I remember looking at the loose-leaf pages. That self, recorded there, I felt no tenderness for her. In fact, she was mortifying, all of her feelings, all of her flaws laid bare, and so I took the notebook out to the pit where we burned the trash and I dropped it in and I dropped in a match or two and watched until it was all gone.

In high school: walking into my bedroom and there was Walker reading my journal. Sex was one thing but this was another way of being naked. Stripped. I took the journal away from him, I took the pages out on to the back porch and burned each one. It became a ritual, the match, the lit cigarette taken to the page, the page curling black, ink turning metallic, ashes crumbling in the tin wastebasket. My past selves silent, safe, mine, and because not recorded, forever mutable.

13

In Susan's tiny apartment, the computer lives under a colorful cloth, a small tablecloth with some kind of map on it. Uncover the computer. Sit in the chair for as long as you like, teacup in both hands, eyes closed. No TV. No Mario Brothers. No NWA. Silence. Maybe a bird in a tree. Maybe the eucalyptus rattle their leaves.

Miss, they say, Miss. My most-at-risk-summer-school-students throw rolls of masking tape and colored pencils across the room to one another. Miss, how do you spell bullet? How do you spell knife? There was a helicopter came to get me, Miss, you want to see the scar?

I threw my enemy's baby on the floor, Miss. I picked her up right out of the stroller. I threw her on the floor. She was the baby of my enemy.

The boys stop tossing the rolls of masking tape. The fan whirs. There is general agreement: when someone kills your brother, something must be done.

Gunfire erupted, they say in the newspapers, gunfire erupted. The girl from my son's high school who beat another girl with a baseball bat says she would do it again. This is what wakes me up at night. I don't need to watch that movie where they leave a dead girl's body on the edge of a river so they can visit her dead eyes. My friends think that movie is brilliant, but I can't watch it.

I threw my enemy's baby on the floor, Miss. She was the baby of my enemy. Do you want to see the scar?

The scar, the literal scar in question, is from a knife, a knife wielded by a child in a different gang. (Indians belong to gangs, one of the graduate students asks me. Isn't that redundant?) And yet, what causes, where is the scar of the white girl who beats the other white girl with a baseball bat? The scars of the students in my university classes who write about anorexia and mothers found drunk in bathtubs and drunk fathers and drug abuse and suicide attempts and car accidents. *"On the subject of my pain. / First of all it is not an object."* All of the students love this poem by Barbara Anderson and, when I read it to them, the scars of the kids at the Shelter come back to me and the scars of the junkies I knew in high school, of the girl I was.

> *I know you think I'm not being specific enough when addressing*
> *the subject of my pain. That I'm not saying Dear Pain:*
> *you are useful in my love.*

The students write their own words on paper, we fold the papers into tiny accordion-fold books, we put the books into small boxes. We paint them. On Fear. The Subject of My Pain. Scars. The Box of the Past. Hope. These are the names of the boxes.

14

The dreamer has come back to the desert. It is now 1992. The doctor has decided on Interferon, an experimental and possibly toxic regimen, for her husband. He has to take it for three months, injections and pills, and if it isn't working, he can quit. But if it *is* working, he has to stay on it for a year. She doesn't know why the idea of the medication itself makes her so sad. Throws her into a panic. He has been sick for years. But now, on the medication, he is visibly ill and she can no longer pretend otherwise. Is this it? She stretches the phone cord all the way into the bedroom and closes the door. She dials a phone number a friend has given her, the phone number of a therapist. She whispers into the phone: my husband is sick, my son is hardly ever home, my daughter is carving the names of boys into her thigh. I can't write. I look ahead of me and all I see is darkness.

15

In the afternoons, the kids and I sit at the table and chop and chop and chop: tomatoes, onions, jalapeños, cilantro, garlic for the pico de gallo. Cabbage. Guacamole. They turn the stereo up. They grate the cheese. I fry the tostadas and tacos in oil so hot it snaps. We eat in the living room at the coffee table, TV on.

After Fernando gives himself his injection and goes to bed, my friend Gloria and I drink margaritas. I let Kathryn and her friend have two wine coolers each. They smoke clove cigarettes out on the front side-walk. (Perhaps this is wrong, but otherwise, everything feels so sad.) We are sitting on the couch. The living room window is open, be-cause of the cooler, but we can still smell the sweet cloying smoke. What are we watching? *In Living Color*? No, that's Sundays. A movie? It must be Friday, then.

When Michael comes home at midnight with his friend Justin, they entertain us. We sit on the couch and they do the running man in slo-mo. They turn the sound off and make up dialog. They are funnier than TV! (Do I realize they are stoned?) They are so hungry! Nachos! Yes! We sit in a circle on the floor and play poker. Pennies from the big jar instead of poker chips. Justin makes us each lick a card and stick it to our foreheads. Everyone else can see it but we cannot. It feels like a third eye. It feels like I am cross-eyed. It feels like I should know something I don't. I touch the salt on the edge of the margarita glass with the tip of my tongue. I don't ever want it to run out.

16

I am the communal mom, the one everyone goes to, the one who listens and makes no judgments. I hear all of the stories the friends tell. About dressing in a red teddy and singing a Christmas song to the guy next door as he works on his car. About a car full of frat boys chasing them and throwing full cans of beer at their car. How Justin rolled down the window, caught the can, and threw it back. And I hear the sad stories, too, about the stepfathers who come into the bedroom in the middle of the night. I think I know all their secrets, I think listening is what a good mother must do, I think listening, knowing what they're *really* doing, knowing so I can give them guidance, I think these are the only ways I can keep them safe. What else can I do? I can't be there all of the time. I can't make their decisions for them.

My two rules are: safety and honesty. Those are my only absolutes. I tell myself that the only things to worry about are the Big Ds: disfigurement, dismemberment, disease, and death. I figure sex is natural, the occasional high, normal. (Just don't drive while doing either.) Am I trying to be the cool mom? No, I think of myself as honest and practical. I figure they *can't* be worse than I was. I figure honesty is the best policy. Really. Can't we just be honest? If I won't admit my mistakes to them, why should they come to me with theirs? I remember how alone I was as a teenager, no one to turn to. I want them to know I am *there*, no matter what. But at night, I worry that I am rationalizing. I worry that I do want to be the cool mom. I wake up in a panic: have I sacrificed their well-being to my own solipsism, my own need to be loved?

I won't know, for years and years and years, that there were secrets, times my own children were vulnerable, threatened, and I didn't know. Why didn't they tell me? I wonder this now. Did they try and I wasn't listening? Maybe, like my mother, I shut my eyes, my ears, my heart.

They must have felt alone.

Why hadn't they come to me? Maybe I passed down to them this fear, down from my mother through me to them: keep what is hidden

hidden. Your secret self is flawed, and if people knew you, the real you, they wouldn't love you. It makes my heart hurt, that I might have done this, that what I tried hardest *not* to pass on, I still did. A silencing of the self. The claustrophobia of needing to please. The inability to ask for help.

17

What I remember is watching Kathryn cross the living room, she has long legs and arms, a perfect oval face, green eyes, feathery eyebrows, a dusting of freckles she hates. She pulls her long hair up into a severe ponytail or lets it loop, heavily, at the back of her head in an impromptu chignon. I remember being in love with her, not being able to separate her from my own past self, my own paralysis of spirit. I should have protected her, I was her mother, but it was like living in the hottest of summers. You stand and blink your eyes: there is no past, no future, only this moment. There is no way to imagine anything outside of the heat, the sun baking your skin, the sun so bright, the asphalt so black, so black it is as shiny as a mirror and in just such a moment, a moment of despair or solipsism, the boyfriend breaks into the house. She is there alone. In this moment, not premeditated, he takes an X-Acto knife to his wrists and slits them. Later that day Michael and Justin will joke that she should have given him a sharper knife, that if he wants to be dead, they can help him be dead, but at the moment, there is blood and she is alone. She puts her arms around him. She leads him out of the house, all the while thinking, please, don't cut me. Please. Ah, we say later, years later, from a philosophical distance, the prerequisite suicidal lover. Everyone has one. But at the time she is only fourteen and in a few weeks, he will send her, from the mental hospital, his driver's license. He must think she'll be able to forget him.

18

The camera was a used 35-millimeter, no light meter or at least no light meter that worked. When the kids were little, I'd taught them about apertures and shutter speeds, taught them to guess, taught them everything is an experiment. Art depends upon chance, I'd told them, but really I just wanted to see through their eyes. They took pictures of the agave in the neighbor's front yard, of my father's hairy ear lobes. They held the camera out at arm's length and took fuzzy self-portraits. Kathryn's gaze was always direct. Her angles askew. But now the crazy boyfriend, released from the mental hospital, stands on the street corner and watches the house, calls at all hours, enlists the sympathies of the mean girls, and they break into the house when Kathryn is alone. She locks herself in my bedroom, they bang on the bedroom door, yell at her to come out. She locks herself in my bathroom, they break down the bedroom door, she contemplates going out the window, but then she would be in the backyard where no one could see. They break a few things, steal a few things, vandalize the kitchen. Afterwards I feel no outrage about this, oddly, although I call the other parents and threaten restraining orders. I don't allow myself to imagine Kathryn, leaning against the bathroom door, looking at that small window, I don't think about the fact that there was no phone in the bedroom, she couldn't call for help, I don't imagine her terrified or angry, I don't imagine what *could* have happened. Instead, I withdraw her from school. I take her with me everywhere, even to the classes I teach at the university, and at night, when she can't sleep, I let her drive me up and down the roads in the desert foothills for hours, windows down, music on, driving therapy, we call it driving therapy. I know all her favorite songs by heart. We will always remember the soundtrack of this particular spring: Beck, I'm a loser, baby. Duran Duran, Ordinary World. Alice in Chains. Nirvana, of course. Hole. Someday you will ache like I ache. I give Kathryn the camera. We buy used darkroom equipment and convert the main bathroom; you have to lean to one side of the enlarger to see yourself as you brush your teeth. At one point, in a fit of uncharacteristic anger, Michael jams his fist into the mirror and cracks it into a web but we wonder if he is really angry or just acting, we can't tell. Sometimes when he's on stage, if we don't know the play, if we don't know his part, we don't recognize him at first. He transforms himself, is able, even physically, to become someone else, and so we wonder, whose anger is he expressing? Instead of buying a new mirror, Kathryn and I create a collage in its place and at its center, the student in front of the tank at Tiananmen Square, a gaunt man dying of AIDS. We buy old books with beautiful black-and-white photographs. We sit on the couch and look at them, run our fingers over the pages as if we can learn their composition by touch. We look at books of collages, Cornell's boxes, we make our own boxes. We marbleize paper in the backyard, buy old poetry journals and fashion magazines, cut out the words and images. She glues them into a black scrapbook. Writes with silver ink in her round cursive a part of her favorite poem, *I have trusted my scarred hands / but they have not been / faithful to me / and sometimes / when they think I am not looking / one of them takes / the other in its arms / whispering hold me hold me / what we wanted was always / beyond our reach / otherwise / we would not have wanted it.* Negatives unfurl from the canister, strips of them hang from the shower rod. Her fingertips swirl the liquid over the exposed paper, the images emerge in the developing tray. There is music, there is silence, the smell of acetic acid, the sound of dripping water, the darkroom as time out of time, breath held, reality suspended and yet crystallized.

19

It was winter in Colorado. My mother was holding my sister. Someone was taking pictures. My shoes were thin and, at the gravesite, I could feel the hard cold earth. This is what comes back to me, floats to the surface, and years after my niece's funeral, when my own children are teenagers, I'll sit at my desk and try to transform this memory into fiction, try to distill my fear of loss and my grief into someone else's story. In fiction, as in life. I wrote to live again, but as a different person, a person who could feel what I had tamped down. Those memories I did not want to remember, when they surfaced, I transformed them into scenes.

It was February 1988 when Michelle died. *How did this happen? Why did this happen?* That's what I kept asking Fernando all the way to Colorado for the funeral. And his answer: these kinds of things happen all the time. Only this time it happened to your family. Fernando never lied to me and for this, I was grateful, but I was in a daze. Not real is what I wanted it to be. And in a way, what was happening, my life at that moment, felt like fiction. I couldn't believe it. I hadn't seen Michelle in four years, since she was an unhappy fifteen, camped out on my couch in Married Student Housing, babysitting for me. I could picture her, then, burning the grilled-cheese sandwiches, closing her lips quickly over her braces when she smiled. I could picture her, even younger, plopping herself down on my mother's couch so she could hold Michael when he was a baby, or younger still, with her sister, their arms churning in pool water, pixie haircuts, pixie smiles. And so since she had not been a presence in my life for years, why this gaping absence? Why couldn't I let myself believe what I wanted: that she was still living in a small apartment with her husband and her tiny son?

I can still hear my mother's voice that night on the phone when she called to tell me: *we have been so lucky, so lucky so far,* her words a prelude to tragedy, as the death of a nineteen-year-old is always tragic, not made worse, although we might feel so, by the fact that she was a mother when she went through the windshield, that her toddler survived, somehow crawled out of his car seat, then out of the car, perhaps through the broken windshield, and was standing by her body when the man who repairs phone lines found them all alone in the Nevada desert.

Okay, those are the facts I always avoid, as well as the cuts on her hands, the fact that her head, her *face*, was completely wrapped when my sister had to identify her. My sister didn't tell me this at the time. No, when I arrived for the funeral, Marilyn held me. She comforted me. She said, what's that I hear? The sound of your heart breaking? It took five or six years for her to tell me that she had to identify Michelle by her hands. And even then, it was almost unbearable. The Lord never gives you more than you can bear, my mother always said and I'd always believed her and it had always comforted me, that I would be able to weather whatever might come my way. But now I was not sure. Did you know? I asked my mother. Did you know that Marilyn had to identify her by her hands? I only hope, my mother said, that the last thing Michelle heard was the baby crying, that she knew he had survived.

And now my children are teenagers. I watch them step into a car and as the car pulls away from the curb, I think, *Wait*.

I sit at my desk. The details from Michelle's funeral become the details in a story I am writing, the minister talks about death as a lioness tearing us asunder, talks about sin, but not about the young man in my story—so not about Michelle—who they were in life, how much they enjoyed it. But there is another layer of memory, here, because the story I am writing is about a friend who died of an accidental overdose when I was pregnant with Michael, and I remembered, when my friend was in a coma, hugging his mother and feeling between us my hard round tummy, Michael swimming inside while just down the hall her son was swimming through layers of consciousness and time and would never wake up, feeling between us her sorrow, the unfairness of the universe because she loved her son and I didn't even know mine.

And so I write and as I write, I physically feel the cold hard earth beneath my feet, its edge and finality. And an hour later, as I'm driving down a street in windy Tucson, on my way to teach a class, I find I am crying. Instead of the cars around me, I see the cemetery I've just described, transposed from that Colorado winter. I see the father of my friend leaning against the limousine, smoking, looking over toward the distant mountains. The father is remembering how he found his son, blue, in the bathroom. How he had to break the door down. And now his child is gone. And people are walking across parking lots, getting into cars, turning the keys in their ignitions. They are driving away as if nothing has happened. Buildings still stand. Birds fly. And he's wondering, shouldn't the world have changed in some way?

20

My mother, when I was pregnant with Michael, said to me: don't expect me to love your child. I have loved too many people and lost them. I don't want to love anyone else.

So this is what she meant, the terror of loving children, and this is why, every night as I am falling asleep, I pray as though breathing, this one word, *please please please.*

2 I

The air at dusk is honey colored, the Catalina Mountains are blue dinosaurs rising from the desert floor, and Michael and Kathryn are flying down Tangerine Road out where the landscape streaming by gets greener and greener with mesquite, where the crooked fingers of the ocotillo are tipped with orange blossoms. They are really flying now, their elbows resting on the open windows of the car. Then they see the place where Michael's friend wrapped his car around a mesquite tree, the place where his car, its tires slipping on a ribbon of sand, flew and wrapped itself around the thick black trunk of a tree and he died. They climb out of the car and kick at the broken glass, it's everywhere, twisted metal, a dented hubcap. There is a strip of chrome glinting in the weeds. Kathryn bends over and touches the wilted flowers other kids have left. Michael reads a few of the notes scrawled across the backs of photographs, holds a necklace in his fingers and then places it back into the glitter of chains and crosses tangled in the mementos at the foot of a homemade cross. Kathryn remembers the last time she saw Dan, it was at the Burger King, he was wearing his black cowboy hat, he was telling her she was heartless. He was laughing. A few nights later, Michael was at the graduation party out in the desert with Dan and his twin brother and all of their friends, and then Dan climbed into the car and it careened into a tree. Kathryn watches her brother, the gold chain slipping from his fingers, the way his face closes down, and she feels like she's taking a photograph. She feels curiously outside all this, outside and inside at the same time.

22

The glass bowl is turquoise, hand blown, and curved like a floppy hat. There are bubbles in the glass. It looks, almost, like water. In it, the strawberries and slices of oranges are beautiful and, outside, even though it's hot, the grass is green and the light filtering through the trees promises a cool evening where the children will be able to play in the backyard and we will be able to sit and watch them without fanning ourselves with paper plates. Fernando's father brings huge submarine sandwiches in boxes as long as the kitchen table. Kathryn makes pico de gallo with jalapeños so hot not even Fernando's brothers will be able to eat it. His sisters bring bowls of macaroni and potato salad. We hang a piñata for the younger children, for later in the evening, right before the cake.

Michael's graduation. I remember sitting in the stands around the football field. I remember the podium where the speaker will stand, where the person conferring diplomas will stand. We were facing north, I think, looking at the mountains, the western light and the shadows it cast falling in a slant across the field as the sun went down. I remember the chairs set up on the field full of bodies in gold and blue gowns. I remember the crush of bodies in the stands, the heat, the lines of people milling, milling, looking for family or friends, scanning the stands. I remember Dan's father holding his hands up in the air as he walked up to accept Dan's diploma and I remember the impossible: my older sister sitting next to me. But my sister couldn't have been sitting next to me. My sister was in Colorado. Maybe it was my younger sister, *her* sorrow I felt, or the sorrow of all those who have lost a child, the heaviness of my own heart, as real as flesh sitting beside me.

There are times when we cannot reconcile heart and mind. Whatever the mind says, the heart says no. I don't believe you. Nothing, nothing can console me.

And yet only a few years later, when Justin's two-year-old daughter is killed in an accident, Dan's father will say, her life was too short, but it was good. We will be sitting at a picnic table, outside the church after the service, we will be eating fruit salad and picking at sandwiches. Kathryn and I will be there and Fernando, who has not been able to cry, not even in the face of this, and Michael and his wife Sara. And Dan's father will say, her life was too short, but it was good. She was always loved, she was always well cared for, she was happy. And because Dan's father is saying this, I will believe it. I will believe this, remember it, hang on to it, and let the fracture of time swallow other memories, the sound of Justin's voice during the service, the way his wife's sobs washed over us and into us and broke our hearts.

23

On the night of Michael's graduation, I remember the piñata as being
blue and gold, but what was it, a cowboy or a superhero? One of Fernando's brothers must have been on the roof, another on a ladder or
in the tree. Or was it Michael in the tree? Or had he gone off with his
friends to Dan's father's house to sit in his quiet backyard? Michael in
the tree, holding the rope to the piñata, this is entirely possible, but he
is wearing, in my memory, a black and white cotton shirt that he had
long since outgrown and so, perhaps, this memory of the piñata be-
longs to an earlier party and perhaps that is why when I see the children standing around, I don't know at first which children they are.
Roseanna looks so much like her older sister Melinda, Joey like his
cousin Marky, Armando like Jimmy. They have been born in waves,
a family population explosion every three years, and so when we see
them, we momentarily think they are their brothers and sisters, their
cousins, or we think they have grown too much too quickly. Mi'jo,
we say, or mi'ja. Andrea, Alicia, Steven, their dark hair, their delighted
eyes. Years later, when their mother dies too young of lymphoma, we
will see her eyes in their eyes. Years later, when we see their children,
our own children will come back to us, we will want to hold them in
our laps. We will want to stroke their hair and kiss their small faces.

24

The video is grainy and, in memory, it seems like it's in black and white, more like an old movie than VHS. Kathryn is in her early twenties, a college student home on break, when we find it. In the video her hair is long and permed and she never looks at the camera. Her boyfriend is holding the camera, I'm sure, and she holds her hand out as if she wants to push him away. She was fifteen or sixteen in the video, we think. We are both surprised by how young she looks. You were just a child! I exclaim to her. Look at you! She shakes her head. I was so young, she says. I can't believe I was ever that young.

Back then I used to joke she was fifteen going on thirty-five. We all thought this—my friends, her teachers, even my mother. Only Fernando didn't see it. She was still his little girl, but she thought he was being sexist. The Hispanic father! Oh, the arguments they had. When Michael was fifteen, she argued, he didn't even have a curfew. And it was true. Fernando's philosophy with Michael was: we have to let him make his own mistakes, now, while we can provide a safety net. But with Kathryn, *No*, he didn't have the same philosophy at all. He couldn't help it; he wanted to protect her. I trust *you*, he told her, it's the world I don't trust.

In the video, there she is, shy and smiling, her long hair in corkscrew curls as was the style, and then there is Nate, her high school boyfriend, the guy we will later refer to as her beautiful fucked-up man because he was both, truly beautiful and truly fucked up. From an alcoholic family, probably abused as a child, in and out of juvenile detention for most of his teenaged years. Damaged. A good heart, but damaged. When the kid in the cell next to him tried to commit suicide, they made him mop up the blood. You could see it in his eyes, the same look of the kids at the Shelter. It meant, love me. Please.

Watching the video, Kathryn laughs. He was *hot*, she says. She waves her hand in front of her mouth as if she is eating chilis. He *was*, I tell her. You didn't want to buy me a cell phone, she says, so you let Nate move in.

And I am awash in guilt. Did I really do that? Let Nate move in? But I did. On the surface, it was not so strange. We had taken Justin in, Fernando had given him a job, and we'd done this with Michael's friend Houston, too. Nate needed a job, a place to stay, and so . . . but this was different. He was her boyfriend. Why on earth did I let him move in? Was it my fear of loss? I felt she needed her own private bodyguard? Or maybe I was afraid she would leave. Or maybe I desperately wanted her to be happy and I thought this would make her happy. I still don't know. That was the worst mistake I ever made in my life, I tell her, the one thing I would take back. She shrugs. I knew what I was doing. I knew how you were.

The odd thing is, even my parents thought it was a good idea. Why were we so afraid for her? And what about dating? We didn't think she should be carefree and dating? Even Fernando's parents seemed to approve. When they heard that Kathryn's boyfriend had moved in, they made the one and only trip across town together they ever made in our whole lives to visit us. They showed up unannounced and sat in the dining room and drank coffee. Nate came in to meet them and he was polite, although he did not sit down and visit, and they went home, satisfied he was a nice boy.

In the video it is the Fourth of July and his brothers are visiting and they videotape each other setting off illegal firecrackers in the desert. My living room is, again, full of teenagers. My house is, again, the house of the multitudes. How long did he live with us, I ask her. Because I don't remember. I don't want to remember. I do remember that she was happy with him only for a little while and then she was unhappy. It took a long time for him to move out, for them to separate from one another. And *then*, she says, laughing, remember? You gave him that old truck so he would leave. That really pissed me off. It was supposed to be *my* truck.

This is why, she says—and although she does not say this on the day we are watching the video, I know it's true then, I know it's true even before she says it—this is why I had to move away. We are too close. It was the only way I could become independent.

2 5

Years later when Kathryn is in her early thirties, my friend Esmé, who is also in her thirties, will tell me about a weekend workshop where the teacher asked them to write about the fairy tale that scared them the most when they were children, the one that scared them or the one they hated, and she had realized, Sleeping Beauty! All of the female characters in my stories are sleepwalking, she says, they need to wake up. We are sitting in a café, eating pizza and drinking wine, and I am talking to her about her stories. It is very muggy in that café and we are both dewy with sweat. I look away from her because my mind has been sent into a drift of its own and I want to follow it. I can't think of one fairy tale that ever mattered to me. I gaze behind the counter where the guy is opening the huge pizza oven with red embers glowing inside and I think *Hades*. Persephone and Demeter. I cannot retell that story without wanting to cry. I understand Demeter. I want her powers. If anyone took my daughter away from me, I would visit permanent winter on the whole world to bring her back.

26

Up to the fifth floor, up a winding stairway so narrow you must put one foot directly in front of the other. In the room, the curtains are dark red. I have been here before in some dream or in an old movie. Open the white wooden shutters and there is a black wrought-iron railing. We are above the sign, Hôtel Gay Lussac. It is summer 2000. We have come to Paris because, again, after months of suffering for nothing, the doctor has said to Fernando, Quit taking it. The Interferon's not working. You ought to go some place you've always wanted to go, the nurse said, to reward yourself for trying. I don't know why, Fernando told me in the car on the way home, but I don't think I'm going to die of hepatitis. Outside the windshield, it had been spring, the paloverdes in bloom, golden. After this second round of Interferon, we've decided that the cure just might be worse than living with the disease.

Across the street from our hotel stands a triangular building, like the Flatiron Building, only white. While Fernando takes his nap — he is worn out from the medicine, skin slightly gray, hair falling out everywhere — I sit in the window and write. On the street level, there are shops, a bakery, *le fromagerie*. Flowers spill out of containers, fruit is stacked in bins, fruit they won't let you touch — *un orange, s'il vous plaît, trois pommes rouges* — the small round grocer chooses fruit for you. Directly across from our window, there are apartments, geraniums in window boxes. A gray cat walks gingerly on the very edge of the steep roof. A man opens his window and smokes a cigarette.

Later, in Nice, a man will walk out on his balcony and water his plants, geraniums, yes, the ubiquitous and beautiful red geraniums, but also a fig or two. The street is so narrow, I could lean out and have a conversation and, in fact, he calls out while I am watching. *Mademoiselle!* he calls to a window to the left and below mine, *Mademoiselle!* he calls with surprising urgency. Below us the waiter is setting green cloths on the tables for dinner.

In the white light of Nice, what do I remember of rainy Paris? Gray and rainy Paris. I remember the Muslim girl with the red headscarf on the steps of the Musée D'Orsay. The knots of schoolgirls along the banks of the Seine. Tourists posing before I. M. Pei's glass pyramid. Police on horseback next to Notre Dame. The black metal sculpture in front of the Holocaust Deportation Memorial, triangular and sharp, I remember this. A single point of light at the end of a long corridor, tiny beads of light on the walls, rows and rows and rows of beads, each representing a person who never returned.

The pizzeria, just around the corner from our hotel in the Latin Quarter, owned by the Egyptian brothers. How could I forget? One strokes his upper lip as if he has a moustache. Mexican? he asks Fernando, *vous êtes* Mexican? And Fernando says, Mexican-American. Mexican, I say, *mais des États-Unis.* And you? Fernando asks, are you French? Oh, the waiter laughs, Egyptian-French. The same. Born here. In France. Between waiting on other tables, he sits with us. Fernando tries Spanish words but the waiter shrugs. In the kitchen, his brother is flipping pizza dough in the air. I thumb through the dictionary, trying to ask the questions Fernando wants to ask and trying to understand the waiter's answers. I point to words, lean over the table to listen, to share with Fernando the chocolate mousse the brother has brought us. I lean across the table for one more bite of chocolate. I trace Fernando's hand with my finger, take another sip of the sweet liqueur and we hear, coming up the street, the music of gypsies.

27

We stop on the bridge, there is a ravine beneath us, but it is a ravine full of trees and birds. Is there a river below? Yes, a sheer drop. We stop on the bridge and look back at the medieval part of Vence, perched there as it has been for hundreds of years, its stone buildings and narrow walkways, windows with boxes of geraniums and tiny roses, the square full of green umbrellas beneath which we sat for lunch. My mother had come here with my older sister some years before, part of a watercolor painting tour; they'd stayed at a hotel in Vence where, every morning, a woman brought a tray with coffee and fresh croissants to their room. *Bonjour!* My mother wanted us to see where she had been and so we've taken the bus up from Nice through the narrow hills, stopping at St. Paul de Vence where Baldwin had lived and died, the stone mosaic walkways, the cemetery where I could not find his name. There is a square in Vence, my mother had told me, the square of the new town, there are shops all along the edges, but you will see a huge tree and an arch and, through there, is the old town. But now we are on the bridge, on our way to find the Matisse Chapel, which is set off in the hills on a narrow residential street, its white floors and white walls and blue and yellow stained glass. The glass casts translucent patches of color, yellow and blue and green, they shift as the sun moves. Also, on the white walls, white tiles with line drawings. Outlines of flowers, outlines of mother and child, the child standing, arms outstretched, already in the shape of a cross. On one wall, the stations of the cross, all in outline, the simplest of charcoal lines. A sketch. Fernando finds this as moving as any cathedral. He fills in for himself, I think, what faith means, as if in this room he has found a kind of spiritual home. Someone else with a clear vision. Outside the windows, the green lawns and gardens.

And then another garden, this one outside of the Chagall Museum. I have never been drawn to Chagall but we walk up from our hotel in Nice, this is another day, perhaps the next day, up through a tunnel marked with graffiti I can't read, through a business neighborhood, stores, their windows and doors closed, perhaps it is a Sunday, trash skittering in a hot wind, a few people watching us, then up winding streets past high walls surrounding mansions, black wrought-iron gates, extensive gardens. We are lost, perhaps, on our way to the Matisse Museum and we find instead Chagall, his paintings. I have never seen them like this, never seen so many in one place, they are so large, so alive with color. I sit on a bench. They are vibrating with color and with multitudes of souls, the layers of images like layers of lives. A palimpsest. Tiny ink-people off in the corners, animals floating, outlines of houses, cities, people huddled below or on the edges of the canvas. Larger souls emerging, floating through the sky, holding onto one another. One is flying on a red horse in a red sky. The vision is not calm, not calming, but passionate and moving, turbulent and earthbound, spirits tied to history, trying to transcend. Here in these visions, the artist is struggling with faith, it seems to me, and I understand: for God so loved the world, I always think, that He made it beautiful and He so loved us that He gave us agency. And what did we do?

28

Vous êtes Mexican? In the south of France they ask us this, too, and in Italy, they motion as if to make a moustache and then shrug their shoulders. Yes, we say, Mexican but *American*. Mexicans from Mexico must not travel very often, I say. Fernando looks at me. It's because we're together, he says. Oh, I say, and I look so British. (Which I do.) Why don't they ask me if I'm British? Why do you get all the attention? And then we're in *Firenze* and the children have joined us and the waiters gather around our table. Yours? They ask Fernando, pointing to Michael and Marcia, Kathryn's dark-haired friend. And then they point to Sara, Michael's wife, who does resemble me, and Kathryn. Yours? They ask me. But when Marcia, who speaks Italian because her parents and grandparents still speak Italian at home, explains that Kathryn is Fernando's daughter, the waiters burst into applause. *Bella*, they tell him with approval, *bellisima!* When we are in other restaurants in other towns, Marcia will eavesdrop. People all over Italy, she tells us, are wondering how we're related. They think we must be one of those "his" and "hers" situations.

No one has ever believed Michael was mine. When he and Kathryn were little, people in the grocery store would say, what beautiful children! They both yours? Yes, I would say. Oh, they must have different fathers! No, I would say, same father. How did that happen, the woman at the grade school asked me. In the usual way, I told her. (How do you think?) But because Kathryn is so fair, she will be asked these questions her whole life. How did you get that last name? Is he your father? Not your stepfather? But he's Mexican. Are you sure? (*Are you sure?! So* you're *Mexican? But only a little, right?*) A Chicana in her Intercultural Perspectives class will tell her, you can't be both. You have to choose. And she'll say: so I can love my Nana but not my Grandma?

After the waiters applaud Fernando for siring Kathryn, he keeps telling me the story. I was there, I tell him. You don't get *all* the credit, I finally tell him. But it is funny. For years, ever since Kathryn turned thirteen, he hasn't wanted to go anywhere alone with her. People stare at us, he says. In the mall. They look at me like, you dirty old Mexican, what are you doing with that young white girl? When Kathryn is about sixteen, she asks Fernando to take her to a Santana concert, but he is in anguish, literally, about walking through the crowds with her. White men and Mexican women, especially, he says, you can't believe the looks. Michael and I joke that we need to get them tee shirts. Fernando's will have an arrow pointing to its left; the lettering will say, "She's My Daughter." Kathryn's will have an arrow pointing to the right; hers will say, "He's My Dad." Then she just always has to stay to his left, Michael says.

We joke about this and then, I swear it's the very same day, we go up to buy bagels. We are in our sweats, Michael is unshaven, he has his arm around me. We stand at the counter, looking at all of our choices. What do I want? he asks me. You want the club sandwich, I tell him. I look up at the woman behind the counter. She has a curious look on her face. He wants a club sandwich, I say. She is still perplexed. I'm supposed to know what he wants, I tell her, I'm his mother. Oh, she says, you're his mother. And then she turns around to the other workers, she's his *mother*, she announces. It is very early in the morning, perhaps I haven't yet had my coffee, or maybe I am just slow, but it isn't until we're in the car that it dawns on me. You don't think they thought, I ask Michael, you don't think they thought we were? Yeah, he says, that's what they thought.

And so it goes. No one believes that Alvarado is Kathryn's last name, but when Michael walks into a store in South Tucson or North Hollywood, they automatically speak to him in Spanish. Kathryn, when white people say things about Mexicans, and they often do, has to declare who she is, *I'm* Mexican, she'll say, although when she's on the Southside, she never feels Mexican *enough*. She will speak Spanish in Spain or Mexico but never in Tucson or L.A. And Michael, in college, when he's shaved his head for a play, gets pulled over in our own neighborhood, gets asked what he thinks he's doing here. Years later, when there's an immigration crackdown in America and Arizona has enacted illegal laws, we'll all joke that Michael and Sara's older son, who is fair like Sara and Kathryn, will be asked, how did you get *that* last name? while his younger brother, who is Michael's clone, will be pulled over and asked for his papers. But how can we joke? About a law that would divide brothers.

29

A table at a sidewalk café in Rapallo. Seaside. *Pizza margherita. Insalata mista.* A carafe of white wine. Coke is just as expensive. A tour bus empties. All around us, the hum of voices, the music of silverware and glasses. We have been to *Firenze*; we'll go to Rome, but Rapallo is our vacation from our vacation, a few days seaside. Moby Dick's. That is the name of the café. There is one waiter rushing from table to table. There are small bowls of black olives. There are families, children in strollers and on tricycles, visiting along the boardwalk in front of the café. Old grandparents gather on the benches. A red Lamborghini—which we will hear later that night as it races through empty curving streets up into the hills above town—is parked in the circle before us. The hills above town are green in the morning. Scattered villas or farmhouses tucked in among the trees. Terraced vineyards. Smoke plumes from burning trash rise in the thin morning air.

My father had died late at night as we were driving Kathryn across the dark desert to her new home near Lake Tahoe. He died alone in his apartment. Heart failure. My sister found him, called me to let me know. The next night, Kathryn and I were sitting on the couch in her living room. The house was an A-frame. Outside the big windows, pinpoints of stars, tall fir trees, snow falling. She was trying to figure out how he could be gone. She looked past me and asked, where *are* you, Granddaddy? Just then, the lights in the dining room behind us went out. She touched my hand. She said, I'm tingling. She said, he's here. It was true. I felt him. His energy surged from her hand into my body where it went straight to my heart, all of his love and all of his sorrow. He was grieving. He wasn't ready to go, but he was saying goodbye.

Twilight is blue. Sara and Marcia get up from the café table and walk down to the water, where they will wait for us. The harbor is dotted with boats just as you have seen in the paintings. Light refracted on blue water. It is the four of us, now, sitting at a table in a café in Italy. It feels like a waking dream. We know we will remember this moment. Kathryn touches my hand, says, it's happening again, the electricity. We all hold hands. In the blue light, molecules are circulating, things unseen can be felt. We all feel him, my father's electricity, his presence. Fernando's fingernails are square, as are Michael's. Kathryn has a small crescent-shaped scar near the corner of her mouth. Michael's eyes are a darker green than hers. I see us as if from a great distance. I see us perhaps from my father's perspective, but I am not floating. I am sitting at the table with my husband; our children are holding our hands.

30

At night, before my mother awakens, I am sitting up in bed. It's as if there is a tether between us. I am tethered to her. I wake up, I help her into the bathroom so that the cord from her oxygen won't get tangled in the wheels of her walker and trip her. Once she is back on her couch in the bedroom, I walk out to the kitchen to get her warm milk and another painkiller. Her townhouse is bathed in soft light from the atrium. The oxygen condenser hums, its red eye unblinking. This is all so familiar, I don't need to be fully awake. I stand in front of her while she drinks the milk and eats two saltines. The pill is her reward. She is so small, as vulnerable as a child even if she weren't in pain. I lift her legs onto the couch where she prefers to sleep, cover her, arrange her old pink cashmere sweater, just so, over her shoulder or over her feet, wherever she feels a chill. When she sees my hand, she looks momentarily confused. Is that my hand or yours, she asks me. Mine, I tell her. I kiss her on the forehead. I crawl back into the double bed she shared with my father.

So it has come to this. The human body, a shell. Has it really come to this? My mother's human body, a shell? I feel like crying. I want my older sister to come and take care of everything. I want to go home and lie next to Fernando, feel him breathing next to me so I can fall asleep. I lie on the edge of my mother's bed, the shadows from the bottlebrush tree fill the room. There must be a full moon. It doesn't make sense, your mother dying. But that is what Fernando tells me. The doctor sent your mother home to die. Without treatment, she will die.

31

In the hospital, that's where she takes both of my hands in hers. She seems almost jubilant, as if we are going to a party. She recites a poem I have never heard before. She is so pleased she remembers all the words, it must be from her childhood. Or maybe it is a song, not a poem but a song, the lyrics about two lovers, about true love, a soldier and his sweetheart, about how they will meet again. No wonder she remembers the words. They are about lovers, but she is singing them for me, to let me know this will not be the last time I see her.

My mother makes me promise to keep Kathryn safe. She's afraid of Prague, the dark sooty land of communists and sex-slave traders, but she does believe in crossing the ocean, in clearing your mind. After all, she put an ocean between my high school boyfriend and me. She left my father by getting on a plane to France. Only by leaving him earthbound, she said, on another continent, could she feel free of his influence. She must have suspected that Kathryn wanted to leave her husband, I hadn't told her, but she must have suspected because she gave her money for the flight. Don't you let her out of your sight for a minute, she tells me, both hands clutching mine. She pauses. But don't you bring her home early. Not even if I die.

We hold hands and we promise. We are not saying goodbye, but this is the closest we will ever come. She has always said, show me you love me. Don't tell me. Words mean nothing. And I have tried to show her, by taking care of her. She has begun introducing me as her devoted daughter — this is Beth, my daughter, she is *devoted* to me — and, here, she inserts some detail about how bossy I am. And even though she is joking — because, really, who ever would have thought we could be so close? so much the same? — it is her way of saying, I know it's been hard for you. I've needed you. I appreciate what you've done. In this moment, I understand her. This is what I should tell her. I understand you. And I understand why it is easier, and means more, to bring a cold cloth and lay it over a child's eyes, easier to sing, to make food, to bring warm milk and medicine in the middle of the night than to speak from the heart.

I am still holding her hands and I say, we are not women who make promises we can't keep. And so we promise. And the odd thing is, I am certain. I am certain the plane will not crash, I am certain Kathryn will not be kidnapped by sex-slave traders, I am certain my mother will not die while I am in Prague.

And, in fact, my mother does not die. Instead she has an operation to stabilize her spine, she is treated for pneumonia and pumped full of morphine which, my older sister says, makes her demented. Because, like my mother, I believe in being incommunicado, I rarely call home. But as I'm sitting in the airless Bohemia Bagel Shop/Internet Café, I open e-mails from Fernando who visits her every day in skilled nursing: *Your mother is recovering. Thinks she's surrounded by Japanese soldiers. Lyn goes home tomorrow. Kay arrives Friday. Love to Kat. To you, too.* When I recite the e-mails to Kathryn and my friend Barbara, I insert the word "stop" wherever there's a period: *Your mother is recovering*—stop—*Thinks she's surrounded by Japanese soldiers*—stop—*Lyn goes home tomorrow*—stop—and my laughter, I hear it, is breathy, almost hysterical. I am so relieved that she is not, for now, my responsibility.

32

Prague. Things to remember: the entryway, the three-sided elevator, the blue living room; the lady across the street in her apartment, tending her window-box garden; Kat's and my room, the explosion of clothes from our suitcases, the red netted curtains beneath the white gauze. Barbara's back bedroom with the leaky ceiling and small porch for drying clothes, gardens with hydrangeas below, apartment balconies across the way. Lunches in the Thai café behind the glass shop, the air molten; the readings at night in the theatre below the smoke-filled bar. Everyone smokes. Le Louvre Café, the garden dining room on the roof, the other buildings around us still taller, so it wasn't as if we were on a roof at all. The Charles Bridge, the light at dusk, honey colored, later blue; the John Lennon memorial; shadowy sculptures of people climbing stairs to a garden as we were saying goodbye to Cynthia after dinner. Sidewalks of small white cobbles, some of which are used in our apartment as window stops; the white inlaid crosses in Old Town Square, twenty-seven, one for each martyr beheaded upon that spot; the clockmaker, blinded so he couldn't go to Germany and make another clock; defenestration, Cynthia tells me, from *fenêtre*, window in French (of course) defenestration, which means to throw someone out of a high castle window, especially during political upheaval, as in a coup. Liquidation, which means only one thing. "In the struggle between yourself and the world, you must side with the world," Kafka said, but I don't think Kafka had children, could have imagined, even in his darkest moments, Terezín, children sent by train to their deaths. Terezín. Kathryn's proof sheets: so many doors, doors behind archways, doors behind bars and grids of bars, interior doors that lead nowhere, long hallways full of doors half-opened, windows behind bars, windows the shape of doors, windows and doors which are not openings, windows and doors which are sealed with heavy iron bars, doors the texture of tombstones, tombstones shaped like doors. Art Brut in the museum that used to be a palace, dream images made by those who were mentally ill, the eyes often haunting or haunted. Tiny tiny obsessive patterns of black ink, figures that could never escape mazes, fragments of photos, crayon, pharmaceuticals, blood. In Art Brut, as in all art, as in Picasso's *Guernica*, there must be a balance, a tension between part and whole, fragmentation and coherence. The discussion of the fragment after Cynthia and Barbara's readings. Barbara arranging chairs on our precarious balcony; Barbara balancing a glass of red wine on the windowsill as she asks me, are we going to accept the terms of the piece or ask the writer to set up new terms?

33

In the hospital room, Kathryn's face is close to my mother's, they are holding hands. Kathryn leans in to whisper so my mother can hear her, and the nurse says to me, Oh, they look so much alike! Your daughter looks so much like your mother. But it is their spirits we see. Kathryn, who saw that brittle was really fragile and so gave my mother what none of the rest of us could, her understanding. When she touches me, my mother told me once, I feel it in her hands. She loves me unconditionally. All of this is what I think and do not say. Kathryn and I have been sitting, each of us on either side of my mother's bed, each of us holding a hand. I have promised my mother that we will abide by her wishes, we will make them remove the breathing tube. I have the strength, I tell her, because of you. I am a strong woman because of you. Her eyes, she closes her eyes then. Rests. She knows I will do what she wants. Fernando's warm hand in the middle of my back at night comforts me. The spirit is of the body. It needs the body. To see, to hear, to touch. This is why every death feels like a kind of violence.

34

When I dream of my mother, I have always abandoned her. In one dream, I am dancing a fox-trot with my aunt and then I notice she is wearing her soft blue bathrobe and then I think, where is my mother? I realize she must be over at the nursing home near St. Joseph's; I realize I haven't been to visit her. I haven't been in a year. In over a year. I haven't even called. I used to call every night. What was I thinking? That just because she's in a nursing home, I don't need to call? I don't need to visit? What if they're not taking good care of her? *She must be so lonely*, this is what I think in my dream, *she must think no one loves her.*

Sometimes I dream about her death. In her eyes, then, there was no pain, just pleading. I had seen it before in my aunt's eyes, *I am so, I am so . . .* Aunt Dorothy had whispered and I'd said, *tired*? And she had nodded her head. In her eyes fatigue, in her eyes pure spirit or pure love, her white hair falling, everything falling, that must be what it feels like. Falling. Letting go.

Do you want us to remove the breathing tube? I was the one who had to ask my mother this. And she had nodded, *yes.* Even though it means we may have to let you go? *Yes.* Are you afraid? *No.* Her last gesture, to comfort us. She raised her head to kiss my brother and sisters and niece, but Kathryn and I were standing at the foot of her bed. We noticed how her head shook with the effort. We wondered why they didn't help her, why they didn't place their hands under her head. We didn't go to get a kiss. I don't know why. Did we think it was too hard for her? Too much to ask? For her to lift her head like that again? Maybe it was because we had already said our goodbyes. Or maybe I thought I would break down, my voice would break. There was such silence in the room. Only her labored breathing. I tried to talk to her. I tried to sing, but I could only hum. I could only hum an incomplete lullaby, a lullaby without a tune, hmmm hmm, hmm hm, the sound of my voice a tether between this world and the next, that is what I wanted to give her, a humming, we are here. You are not alone. Helping someone die feels like giving birth, the same held breath, the same pushing from one world to another. Let go, Mom, you can let go. It's okay. That's what I hummed.

Sometimes in my dreams, I feel her hand in mine. We are sitting at the table of my childhood. She doesn't want me to leave. I tell her I just want to walk around outside. Just for a minute. To walk around outside in the sunlight. I'll be right back, I tell her. Her hand in mine, it feels so real, her thin papery skin, so smooth. And then I remember. She's dead. She says, I miss you. I say, I miss you, too, Mom. How *are* you? (I think to ask.) Are you okay? Oh, I'm okay, she shrugs, she's sitting in her wheelchair now. But I'm surprised, she says, you haven't cried very much. And I say, Oh, *Mom*, you know how *that* is.

35

On the other side of the street, a woman in a dark green jogging suit and black boots is smoking a cigarette and talking on a cell phone. She has on big sunglasses and a thin scarf wrapped around her neck, the ends thrown over one shoulder. Every now and then, as she paces, she gestures emphatically with the cigarette. It's one of those drab winter no-sky days in California where the cloud cover is like a low gray ceiling held up by date palms, the caryatids of Los Angeles. I am rocking my grandson in the slider, the creak creak the only noise besides my throaty humming. He is studying my face as intently as I am studying his. He reaches out a hand to touch my lips and I take it in my own hand, slip my thumb under the curl of fingers. He grasps. I have come to help in this, the busiest time of year for Michael and Sara and, of course, I have caught William's cold. Dear little germ factory. It is so quiet for L.A., only the sound of his breathing and an occasional car passing or a shout from teenagers as they slouch home from school. I close my eyes, hoping he will close his, and compose little paragraphs in my mind. These little paragraphs are very beautiful, stuffed with the stuff of life. *The past, to repeat the words of Proust, is hidden in some material object. To wander about in the world, then, is also to wander about in ourselves. That is to say, the moment we step into the space of memory, we walk into the world.* And so it is. I walk into the world. These little paragraphs are perhaps too beautiful, too sad, but what is to be done, I wonder, as I sit with William in my arms. What is to be done? I drift, I drift. At home, Kathryn and Fernando are making Christmas tamales, my cell phone on vibrate next to me, in case they call again. How much salt? How long on the stove? Although Kathryn knows—she has made tamales with me since she was a child—Fernando is not sure, wants me to tell him exactly how his mother made them. It is dusk there, the light tawny in Tucson at dusk, the tangerines incandescent in that light, glowing on the trees, suspended in impossible longing.

References

Page 6, Nicolas Abraham from "Notes on the Phantom: A Complement to Freud's Metapsychology," as quoted in *A Family of Strangers* by Deborah Tall, Sarabande Books, 2006.

Page 44, Anne Carson from "Anthropology of Water," in *Plainwater*, Knopf, 1995.

Page 44, Pico Iyer from "Why We Travel," *Salon*, March 18, 2000.

Page 117–118, James Baldwin from "Uses of the Blues," in *Playboy*, October 1964.

Pages 131–132, Barbara Anderson, "On the Subject of My Pain," from *Junk City*, Persea Books, 1987.

Page 139, Richard Shelton, "My Hands Are My Enemies," from *The Bus to Veracruz*, University of Pittsburgh Press, 1978.

Page 167, Paul Auster from "The Book of Memory" in *The Invention of Solitude*, Penguin, 1982.